The Politics
of Sentiment

RICHARD E. SINCERE, JR., is assistant to the president for research at the Ethics and Public Policy Center. He received a B.S. in foreign service from Georgetown University, where he was also a member of the faculty of the Summer Forensics Institute. He serves on the board of directors of the American Civil Defense Association. His articles have appeared in more than a dozen periodicals.

LUCY MVUBELO is the general secretary of the National Union of Clothing Workers, the largest black trade union in South Africa, and has long been associated with anti-apartheid and pro-labor activities. She has represented black women workers at the International Labor Organization in Geneva, Switzerland.

The Politics of Sentiment

Churches and Foreign Investment in South Africa

Richard E. Sincere, Jr.

Foreword by Lucy Mvubelo

**Ethics and Public Policy Center
Washington, D.C.**

Library of Congress Cataloging in Publication Data
Sincere, Richard E.
    The politics of sentiment.

    Bibliography p.
    Includes index.
    1. Investments, Foreign—South Africa—Moral and
ethical aspects.   2. South Africa—Race relations.
3. World Council of Churches.   I. Ethics and Public
Policy Center (Washington, D.C.)   II. Title.
HG5851.A3S56   1984   332.6'73'0968   84-28642
ISBN 0-89633-088-5

$8.00

Bishop Tutu, I want to ask you a . . . question. I do not understand how your Christian conscience allows you to advocate disinvestment. I do not understand how you can put a man out of work for a high moral principle.

You and I both know well the parable of the sheep and the goats, and we know well the importance that Jesus attached to the feeding of the hungry and the giving of water to the thirsty.

You could put a man out of a job and make his family go hungry so that some high moral principle could be upheld.

It would go against my own deepest principles to advocate anything that would put a man—and especially a black man—out of a job.

Therefore I cannot understand your position.

I think your morality is confused just as was the morality of the church in the Inquisition, or the morality of Dr. Verwoerd in his utopian dreams. You come near to saying that the end justifies the means, which is a thing no Christian can do.

—ALAN PATON
Johannesburg Sunday Times
October 21, 1984

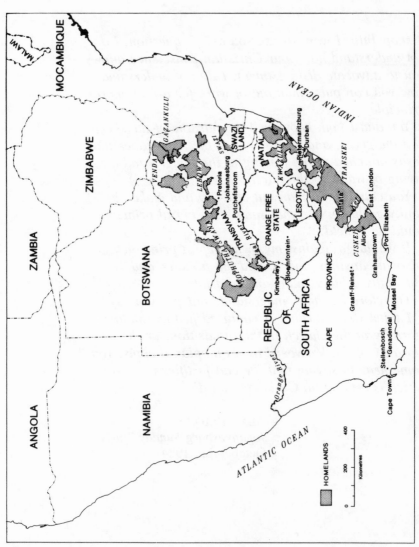

Contents

(Continued on next page)

Foreword

By Lucy Mvubelo

THIS IS AN IMPORTANT BOOK on an important question. The issue of external investment in South Africa is one that deeply affects all of us who live in this beautiful, paradoxical, and complex land. By the same token, disinvestment will be felt by all of us—black, white, Asian, or colored. The question is also important to Americans because it affects relations between the United States and South Africa, relations that in turn have an impact upon peace, prosperity, and stability throughout Africa.

I am a worker and trade unionist living in Soweto who knows how the ordinary African worker suffers under the discriminatory effects of apartheid. I want fuller participation by my black co-workers and all groups in the economy and political system of my beloved country. I have heard all the arguments and proposals for changing our internal situation through external pressures to isolate South Africa from the Western democracies, but I am not convinced.

To proponents of isolation, disinvestment, and embargoes, I must say: Don't break off contact, and don't advocate disengagement and withdrawal of foreign investments. Only indigenous movements—the trade unions, the political groupings, the schools, the business associations—within South Africa can bring about significant, positive change. Outsiders can influence it, but only through participation, not by isolation.

Foreign investment has created jobs for thousands of African workers who would otherwise be unemployed. Thanks to the policies of foreign firms operating here, black workers have gained significant wage increases, often larger than the increases gained by black workers in South African companies. These workers enjoy the benefits of equal-opportunity codes adopted by American and European firms, whose example is now being followed by many South African companies. The vitality of South Africa's economy offers more hope to South African blacks than destructive forms of pressure from abroad.

Unlike so many Africans throughout the continent and in South Africa itself who still live in dire poverty, middle-class blacks own a home, a television set, perhaps a car or a washing machine. These people and others who aspire to a similar standard of living now have a stake in peaceful reform, which does not mean that they will not continue to agitate forcefully for their rightful voice in political, social, and economic affairs. By insisting on the withdrawal of foreign companies—even of only American firms—disinvestment advocates are asking a substantial number of black workers to sacrifice their jobs, to sacrifice their only realistic means of attaining wider opportunities and higher living standards.

This book is important because it examines the statements of Christian churches in America and elsewhere outside South Africa. The churches have taken the lead in the international struggle against apartheid. Unfortunately, church leaders are often misguided and often ill informed, and their statements and activities remain unexamined in light of the actual conditions in South Africa.

Those who insist that Christian vision requires them to support revolutionary change in South Africa fail to acknowledge any reform in South Africa and fail to see—or turn a blind eye to—the effects violent revolution will have. My friends, colleagues, and co-workers in South Africa are deeply concerned to learn that foreigners think South Africans can live better in an economy laid waste by an investment boycott.

The Ethics and Public Policy Center in Washington, D.C., is a research organization committed to the rule of law, human rights, and peaceful change. I commend the Center for bringing together in this book the views of the American churches and the World Council of Churches and comparing them with the views of churches and church leaders here in South Africa. This gives the reader a chance to see how the uninformed view from a distance contrasts with the facts as we know and experience them.

I hope this careful study will dissuade well-meaning, compassionate, and thoughtful Americans from pressing for shortsighted laws calling for divestment and disinvestment. Such laws will set back the cause of human rights and peaceful change. They will hurt the South African economy and the very persons their advocates seek to help.

Preface

THE IDEA FOR this study was born five years ago. Pursuing his persistent interest in economic development and human rights in the Third World, Ernest W. Lefever, president of the Ethics and Public Policy Center, visited the Republic of South Africa in 1979 to ascertain first-hand the views of church leaders there on the vexing problem of external investment, its impact on the economy, and its probable effects on the larger struggle for political participation by all the peoples of that diverse and troubled land. He interviewed representatives of many denominations and all of the country's major racial groups—black, colored, Asian, and white.

After some reflection, Dr. Lefever decided that a comparative analysis of views on the investment issue from inside the country and from abroad would throw light on both applied Christian ethics and current public policy. So he commissioned a study by several scholars of pronouncements by churches in the United States, by the World Council of Churches, and by churches in South Africa.

Five years later and after more than the usual writing, rewriting, and editing involving half a dozen persons on three continents, *The Politics of Sentiment: Churches and Foreign Investment in South Africa* has emerged. The phrase "politics of sentiment" might seem purely pejorative, suggesting the making of policy by sentiment rather than by reason grounded in empirical data. Certainly this kind of policy advice is given, especially among well-meaning people. Wishful thinking and noble slogans frequently beguile men of good will into espousing utopian programs that may worsen rather than better the problems they address.

Yet sentiment also has a positive and constructive role in politics, if sentiment can be taken to mean fidelity to certain basic values—justice, freedom, order, and respect for the human person. Politics without this kind of sentiment is cruel; politics based only on sentiment invites chaos. The tragic history of the twentieth century shows that revolutionary slogans, however noble they sound, often lead to tyranny. As Joseph Conrad put it, "the revolutionary spirit is mighty convenient in this, that it frees one from all scruples as regards ideas."

This is not a book about apartheid. It is a study of whether foreign investment in South Africa helps or hinders the cause of greater justice for the people of all races there. Its intention is to provide facts, facts about the economic and political situation in South Africa but primarily about what church leaders and bodies have said on the question of external investment.

I would like to thank the many people who helped with this study at early or later stages. Among those who wrote partial early drafts, provided memoranda or information, or commented on portions of the manuscript are John Chettle, Philip Christenson, E. Stephen Hunt, Dirk Kunert, Albert Menendez, John Montgomery, Joseph A. O'Hare, S.J., Arnt Spandau, William Stemper, and Timothy Wheeler. A number of church officials, both here and in South Africa, were kind enough to answer my queries about official statements on investment; they provided some of the essential data for this book. Special thanks go to Lucy Mvubelo, who agreed to contribute the foreword even though her home had only recently been firebombed by radical terrorists who were targeting moderate black leaders. For her courage in the face of strife and danger, we salute her.

This study could not have come to fruition without the knowledge and guidance of Dr. Lefever, who gave me the first segment of the assignment (the U.S. churches) four years ago. That task eventually broadened to include the whole study. Without Dr. Lefever's theoretical understanding, insistence on precision, and first-hand exposure to South African realities gained over two decades, this would have been not a book but a mishmash of quotations, disjointed concepts, and hasty conclusions.

As usual with Center publications, the reader will be indebted to Carol Friedley Griffith for her editorial fine tuning. For any errors that remain, I take full responsibility. The facts selected and conclusions reached are mine.

RICHARD E. SINCERE, JR.
Ethics and Public Policy Center

Washington, D.C.
December 1984

CHAPTER ONE

A Political, Economic, and Moral Issue

ON SEPTEMBER 15, 1984, State President Pieter W. Botha spoke at the opening session of South Africa's first multi-racial parliament. Noting the exclusion of the country's 17 million blacks from the national government, he said: "Democratic political participation must also be further extended among our black communities . . . to ensure their advancement and to meet the demands for justice." Means would be found, he said, to permit blacks to participate "in political decision-making in matters affecting their interests."[1]

Less than a year earlier, in November 1983, white South African voters had approved a new constitution by a vote of nearly two to one. The constitution provides the first opportunity for parliamentary representation by non-whites. The new parliament has three chambers: one for white representatives, one for coloreds (persons of mixed race), and one for Asians (in South Africa this means mainly Indians). The three houses will together consider legislation that concerns them all (such as foreign policy) and will separately consider matters particular to each group (such as their separate school systems). A new office, that of state president, elected indirectly by the three chambers, was created, combining the two previous offices of president and prime minister. As state president, Botha will have significantly greater powers than he did as prime minister under the Westminster system inherited from Britain.

Response to the new constitution was mixed in South Africa and abroad. Chief Gatsha Buthelezi, leader of the six-million-member Zulu nation and one of South Africa's most respected black leaders, condemned the constitution as a permanent institutionalization of apartheid. The Southern African Catholic Bishops' Conference had

1

advised Catholics to vote against it, and expressed dismay at its passage. Bishop Desmond Tutu, general secretary of the South African Council of Churches, condemned the new constitution as "a sly piece of work based on race intended to entrench white minority power."[2] The *New York Times* editorialized: "To call the reform tokenism is to flatter it."[3]

The *Washington Post,* however, expressed guarded optimism: "Will the South African government take the vote as a mandate for further change—for what might better be called real change, change granting genuine political rights to all South Africans? The only thing more foolish than giving Pretoria credit for something it has not yet done would be to rule out all possibility that the new constitution can yet make some contribution to the cause."[4] The *Economist* of London said the constitution had "become a precondition for advance . . . a recognition—regarded as such by Afrikaners of both left and right—that the whites can no longer claim wholly exclusive political rights."[5]

Many other persons in South Africa and the West also saw in the new constitution hope for further reform. Some even suspected that the National Party government, which had pushed hard for its acceptance, had a "secret agenda" to bring urban blacks—those who live and work in the cities while holding "citizenship" in the rural "homelands"— fully into the political process in the near future.

That over 65 per cent of the South Africans who voted approved the new constitution showed a widespread willingness to change. The addition of the 10 per cent who voted against it for not going far enough suggests that three-fourths of white South Africans favor reform. The vote was a severe blow to the far right, whose parties demand stringent adherence to racial segregation and permanent denial of enfranchisement for blacks.

The first elections for non-whites under the new constitution took place in August 1984. Despite demonstrations, student strikes, boycott threats, and some violence, substantial minorities of both coloreds (30 per cent) and Indians (20 per cent) voted. The Reverend Allan Hendrickse, leader of the (colored) Labour Party and a long-time opponent of apartheid, and Amichand Rajbansi, leader of the (Indian) National People's Party, became the first non-whites to hold cabinet positions in the South African government when their parties won majority control of their chambers.

Opponents of the 1983 constitution formed a coalition, the United Democratic Front (UDF), which called for a boycott of the colored and Indian elections. Leaders of the UDF include the Reverend Allan Boesak, a Dutch Reformed Church minister who is president of the World Alliance of Reformed Churches. Both sides in the debate—participants in and opponents of the constitutional arrangements—agree that regardless of what else happens, the South African political picture has been irreversibly altered.

THE POLITICAL AND RACIAL SETTING

The Republic of South Africa is about two and a half times the size of Texas—or the size of West Germany, France, Italy, Belgium, and the Netherlands combined. The strategic value of its location at the southern tip of the African continent has been recognized since the 1650s, when the Dutch government sent Jan van Riebeeck to the Cape of Good Hope to establish a food-and-supplies station for ships sailing between Europe and the East Indies.

The 25 million people of South Africa come from many racial and ethnic groups. *Blacks* number about 17 million. The largest black tribe or nation is the 6 million Zulus; other large ones are the Xhosa, Tswana, and Sotho peoples. The 4.5 million *whites* include descendants of the original Dutch and French Huguenot settlers and of the British colonial rulers of the eighteenth and nineteenth centuries, and more recent immigrants from Europe, America, and other parts of Africa; the largest group of whites is the Afrikaners, of Dutch descent. "*Coloreds*," numbering 2.6 million, are persons of mixed-race ancestry; most of them live in the Cape Province. Virtually all of the 806,000 *Asians* are descendants of Indian workers brought to the country in the late nineteenth century to work on sugar plantations in the province of Natal. The predominant languages in South Africa are English and Afrikaans, the latter derived from seventeenth-century Dutch with borrowings from Malay and native African languages. Numerous indigenous "Bantu" languages and dialects are spoken also.

South Africa's history of settlement and development is similar to that of the United States and Australia: the original European settlers found a barren, undeveloped, largely unpopulated land and brought it into the modern era through hard work, determination, suffering, and, often, luck. The white settlers came into conflict with small groups of aborigines—the Khoikhoi, whom they called Hottentots; the San, whom they called Bushmen; and, eventually, the Bantu, blacks, who were migrating toward the Cape, where the whites had already settled. Frontier wars, including massacres of blacks by whites and whites by blacks, marked the first two hundred and fifty years of South African history.

During the nineteenth century, Britain increased its territorial holdings in South Africa. The resentment of Dutch settlers toward these British incursions resulted in the Boer War of 1899-1902, in which Britain defeated the Dutch settlers of the Transvaal and the Orange Free State, who called themselves "Boers" (Dutch for "farmer") or "Afrikaners." Less than a decade later, in 1910, Britain granted the colony autonomy in its own affairs, and in 1961 South Africa became an independent republic.

Although South Africa's government is sometimes characterized as oligarchic or authoritarian, it is, according to Freedom House (a New York–based human rights organization), "a parliamentary democracy in which over 80 per cent of the people have been excluded from participation in the national political process because of race."[6] Even with the constitutional changes of 1983-84, two-thirds of the populace is denied the right to vote in national elections. From the ascendancy of the pro-apartheid National Party in 1948 until 1983, only whites could vote and only whites could run for parliament. (Until 1968, however, coloreds were able to elect white legislators chosen to represent their interests in parliament. And at various periods, especially in the Cape Province, certain blacks were also granted a limited right to vote for white candidates.) Freedom House adds that there is a "limited scope for non-whites to influence affairs within their own communities."

Even under the 1983 constitution, multi-racial political parties are not permitted. Nevertheless, lively political debate takes place within and among all racial groups, and both black and white South Africans express their views in a press that is among the most free in Africa.

The best known and most controversial feature of South African politics and government is the practice of apartheid, which in Afrikaans means "apartness." This separation (or segregation) of the races takes two forms. Petty apartheid is simple segregation, similar to that which existed in much of the United States prior to the civil rights movement of the 1960s. Blacks and whites live in separate neighborhoods, attend separate schools, and use separate rest rooms and water fountains in public places. Certain jobs may be reserved for whites or blacks only. Blacks must carry identification documents, or "passes," with them at all times. When questioned by police or other officials, blacks must produce these documents to prove they have permission to live or work in certain areas, such as major cities. Without such proof, they may be forced to move to a rural "homeland."

  Separate development, sometimes called "grand apartheid," is a much more complex and controversial concept. Under it, the Pretoria government intends to separate black South Africans from the Republic of South Africa and grant them citizenship in independent states drawn along traditionally recognized tribal or national boundaries. Critics of this policy charge that the lands granted the black national states are resource-poor and overcrowded, and that despite the official policy, the states will continue to be economically and politically dependent on South Africa. Indeed, boundaries have been drawn in such a way that some of the best farmland remains in white hands even if it means the states are broken up into non-contiguous pieces; of the ten national states, only tiny Qwaqwa consists of a single block of territory. So far, four of these "homelands"—also called Bantustans—have been granted independence: Transkei, Venda, Bophuthatswana, and Ciskei. Several others have been given autonomy in internal affairs. No government other than Pretoria has yet recognized the independent homelands.

  The stated purpose of separate development is to provide each South African with citizenship according to his racial ("national") group, and eventually to develop a "constellation of states" in southern Africa that will cooperate in common concerns of economic development, natural resources, agriculture, and regional security. Critics argue that separate development condemns the black majority to citizenship in resource-poor, economically unviable homelands, and that it is designed to perpetuate white minority rule and white dominance over the country's wealth.

South Africa's Strategic Value

For nearly 400 years the Cape of Good Hope has served as a major supply station for ships traveling from Europe and America to the Middle East and Asia. It stands guard over the strategic ocean routes for oil tankers from the Persian Gulf and Indonesia to Western Europe, and for ships carrying goods to and from Europe and the Far East. South Africa's naval base at Simonstown is the largest naval facility in the southern hemisphere. In a war involving the navies of the super-powers, Simonstown would be of prime importance.

The country's strategic importance lies not only in its location but also in its mineral resources. According to a 1981 report by the Study Commission on U.S. Policy Toward Southern Africa, sponsored by the Rockefeller Foundation, the republic has the world's largest known deposits of chromium, manganese, platinum, vanadium, and gold—all vital for industrial use—and major reserves of many other valuable minerals, including asbestos, coal, copper, diamonds, iron, nickel, phosphates, silver, uranium, and zinc.[7] Richard Nixon noted that the resources of South Africa and its neighbors constitute "a mineral treasure of almost incalculable strategic and economic importance."[8] Soviet president Leonid Brezhnev proclaimed: "Our aim is to gain control of the two great treasure houses on which the West depends—the energy treasure house of the Persian Gulf and the mineral treasure house of central and southern Africa."[9]

Aspects of the South African Economy

The industrial democracies depend heavily on South Africa as a source of these strategic minerals. The United States, Canada, and European countries all have other substantial economic interests there also. Foreign trade and investment constitute a major portion of South Africa's economy; importing and exporting account for more than half of its gross domestic product (GDP). Foreign investment in the country's economy (as of 1979) was $26.3 billion, or 20 per cent of the value of its industrial capacity. Of that $26.3 billion, 80 per cent was held by five countries—Britain, West Germany, France, Switzerland, and the United States.[10] Total European investment in the country is nearly four times greater than the U.S. investment, however, and European Economic Community trade with South Africa is three times greater than that of the United States.

South Africa also has extensive economic ties throughout southern Africa. It has investments in most of the other ten countries of the region (the exceptions are Angola and Tanzania). It provides develop-ment aid to most of its neighbors and cooperates in ecological and agricultural efforts with them. South African trade with other African states amounts to more than $1 billion each year, primarily in foodstuffs but also in manufactured goods and industrial equipment. South Africa provides the base of a transportation network that unites most of southern Africa and gives all countries in the region outlets for trade with the rest of the world. According to at least one observer, the "economic and general interdependence" of the area seems greater in 1984 than it was twenty years ago.[11]

Of the fifty African states, South Africa is the only substantially industrialized one. In 1978 its share of the continent's economic output was 20 per cent; in this it was second only to Nigeria, which has vast oil reserves and a population three times as large. South Africa's share of the overall industrial output was 40 per cent. It produced 86 per cent of Africa's steel and more than 50 per cent of its electrical power. Not surprisingly, in view of its economic dominance, South Africa enjoys the highest per capita income, standard of living, and life expectancy in Africa. (Life expectancy in South Africa, as of 1978, the latest year for which firm figures are available, was for whites 73 years, Indians 64, coloreds 57.5, and blacks 59.4. By comparison, Ghanaians had a life expectancy of 45 years, Ethiopians 40, and Nigerians 36.[12]) Though high for Africa, South Africa's standard of living does not begin to match those of the United States, Western Europe, and Japan. Appendix A compares South African per capita income to those of other developing countries and some industrial states.

South Africa straddles the economic fence between the First and the Third World; in some ways it can still be considered a developing country.[13] Many black South Africans continue to be hungry in a land of plenty; at the same time, a substantial black middle class has developed and is growing. Poverty is prevalent in the homeland areas, though South Africa as a whole compares favorably to other African states in poverty level. Substantial portions of the country are undeveloped desert lands, dotted with subsistence farms. South Africa has 12.5 per cent of the land area of the United States and about 11 per cent of the U.S. population; yet its 1981 gross domestic product amounted to only $74.4 billion, or 2.6 per cent of the U.S. GDP.[14]

Most rural blacks are poor, and many go to the cities to seek employment. The Group Areas Act (a law that governs ownership and habitation in specified geographic regions according to race), the Pass

Laws (a system of internal passports applicable to blacks only), and other "influx controls" are designed to prevent an overwhelming movement from country to city.[15] The government has also responded to this migration by forcibly resettling blacks from the cities and other "white areas" to the homelands. Influx-control laws have sometimes been cited as justification when black farmers were forced to leave their homes on land their families had owned for generations and resettle in the homelands. The *South Africa Foundation News* noted that a national research project on relocation, the Surplus People Project, had estimated in 1983 that over a twenty-year period, there had been 3.5 million removals. (Since some persons were moved more than once, fewer than that number of people were relocated.) Between 1960 and 1980, the project reported, the proportion of the black population that lived in the homelands rose from 40 to 54 per cent. Most of the relocations, it appears, were involuntary, and sometimes the authorities used violent coercive measures. Conditions are in general worse in the resettled areas than in the townships and villages left behind, especially in terms of hygiene and sanitation, economic viability, and transportation.[16] This is particularly true of resettled areas that are distant from cities.

Because of the country's resource base and its economic ties to the Western democracies, the prospects of both economic and political gains for blacks are good. Soweto, the large black suburb of Johannesburg, boasts several millionaire black businessmen. The town has homes costing $65,000 and more, and small businesses owned by blacks are flourishing. Black income has risen rapidly in recent years—one estimate by General Motors puts black wages in general at 55 per cent of white wages in 1980, up from 20 per cent ten years earlier.[17] The black middle class now numbers more than two million, approximately 12 per cent of the black population. This growing economic power, plus the growing need for skilled workers in the mining and industrial sectors of the economy, leads black and white business leaders to predict fuller political participation for urban blacks in the not-too-distant future, since a rise in economic power typically leads to an increase in political power. Gavin Relly, chairman of the Anglo American Corporation, South Africa's largest business enterprise, has pointed out: "If you want a viable capitalist system, you can't make rules that restrict people's full enjoyment of the system."[18]

Relly and other South African businessmen have lobbied heavily for the repeal of influx-control laws, both because they are inequitable and because they restrict the flow of labor and thus obstruct economic growth.

Summing up the prospects for change in South Africa, Harvard political scientist Samuel P. Huntington observed: "The relatively high level of economic development by African standards, the intense contestation that occurs within the minority permitted to participate in politics, the modest expansion of that minority to include the coloreds and Asians, and the influence of Western democratic norms, all provide a basis for moving in a more democratic direction. However, that basis is countered on the other side by the inequalities, fears, and hatreds that separate blacks and whites."[19]

THE INVESTMENT-DISINVESTMENT DEBATE

South Africa's extensive economic and political ties with the West have made its racial policies the subject of greater Western scrutiny and criticism than they would otherwise encounter. Both critics and supporters of apartheid recognize that basic changes must occur. The difficult questions are: What changes, and how fast?

The underlying premise of this study is that constructive change is politically necessary, morally desirable, and historically possible, but that the change must be initiated and carried out by the people of South Africa, not by outsiders. This premise stems from the principle of non-interference in the domestic affairs of other states observed by the United States and enshrined in international law, including the United Nations Charter. Change must also be constructive, timely, and peaceful.

The purpose of this study, however, is not to address the merits of various routes to greater social justice in South Africa, nor to examine the wide range of problems inherent in the quest for justice in a multi-racial, multi-cultural, multi-lingual society. Its purpose is more limited—to evaluate one of several tactics by which outsiders have attempted to stimulate change in South Africa.

A fundamental term in the South Africa debate is *disinvestment,* the withdrawal of foreign corporate investments from the country. The principle of disinvestment also includes preventing further investment, prohibiting the purchase of gold Krugerrand coins, and terminating foreign bank loans to the government or corporations in South Africa. Related terms are *divestment,* in which stockholders—either individuals or institutions like colleges and churches—sell their stocks in corporations with holdings in South Africa or withdraw their funds from banks that make loans there; and *disengagement,* a broader concept that includes diplomatic, cultural, and economic sanctions against South Africa, arms embargoes, and trade boycotts, and may include both disinvestment and divestment.

Here we are concerned primarily with *disinvestment,* which has become the watchword of much of the anti-apartheid movement outside South Africa. In an effort to draw attention to the investment issue, several U.S. cities—including Washington and Philadelphia—and states (Connecticut, Maryland, Massachusetts, Michigan, and Nebraska) have passed laws barring the investment of government-controlled monies, such as public-employee pension funds, in banks or corporations that do business in South Africa. Although the constitutionality of such laws has been questioned,[20] many other city councils and state legislatures are considering similar proposals.

This study will deal particularly with the views of religious leaders and bodies on disinvestment. We will examine the World Council of Churches (chapter 2), churches in South Africa and the South African Council of Churches (chapter 3), and American churches and ecumenical organizations, including the National Council of Churches (chapter 4). Chapter 5 will assess South Africa's economy and politics. The final chapter will evaluate the recommendations of the churches in terms of their stated objectives and their probable impact on South Africa's economic and political development.

Differing Approaches to South Africa

To South Africa's bitterest enemies, the present system appears to perpetuate racism, capitalism, and exploitation at their worst; to many of South Africa's friends and supporters, the present system, though making significant reforms, seems to teeter on the edge of political instability and is vulnerable to subversion and terrorism. Both sides believe that social and political change is necessary to maintain (or achieve) peace, order, and greater justice in that country and southern Africa generally.

Here as elsewhere there are two basic conceptions of how political change should come about: by *evolution*, or by *revolution*.

Evolution is the preferred course of those who espouse "constructive engagement" with South Africa, the position taken by most Western powers. A leading spokesman for this view is Chester Crocker, assistant secretary of state for African affairs in the Reagan administration, who articulated the concept in a widely read *Foreign Affairs* article in 1980.[21] Dr. Crocker has argued that "pulling out of South Africa, whether it's investment or trade relationships or whatever, is not going to accomplish any predictable objective, except maybe to make us feel a little bit less involved and a little bit more pure."[22] Advocates of disengagement, he said, want to "walk away from the dilemmas of change" rather than getting involved in change.[23]

This official view was underscored in June 1983 by Lawrence S. Eagleburger, undersecretary of state for political affairs. "The United States proceeds from the conviction that our national interest and the interests of the West demand an engagement—constructive and peaceful—in the affairs of southern Africa," he said. "The implications are clear. If we wish to shape events, we must be prepared to take initiatives, make investments, support those things we believe in, build institutions and bridges. We must, in short, be involved."[24]

Secretary of State George P. Shultz said in February 1984: "Economic development itself is a powerful engine for social and political evolution. . . . Those who advocate disinvestment and economic sanctions would pull the rug out from under those South Africans who have taken the first concrete steps toward a . . . more equitable society. . . . We should recognize our limits: we can support and encourage change, but we cannot replace local initiative, institutions, and vision."[25]

Revolution, the complete overthrow of the South African regime, is the course of action preferred by some political and religious organizations in the West and in South Africa. Proponents of drastic change do not always advocate violence, though that is usually a natural extension of their approach. All revolutionaries, however, demand radical political change, beginning with immediate control of the government in Pretoria by the black majority. They hold that the white South African regime is the greatest violator of human rights and dignity in the world today. They demand the isolation of South Africa from the rest of the world and call for economic sanctions against it. Among those holding these views are a substantial number of religious activists, many with ties to the World Council of Churches and the (U.S.) National Council of Churches. Some of these groups have sent material aid to terrorist groups that seek to destabilize and overthrow the white-controlled government.

Those who favor revolutionary change are likely to favor disinvestment as a tactic. Most supporters of disinvestment believe that (1) South Africa is the worst violator of human rights in today's world (some consider it worse than even Nazi Germany and Stalinist Russia); (2) the volume of U.S. investment in South Africa is considerable; (3) U.S. investment supports the apartheid regime; (4) external pressure can induce political change; and therefore (5) withdrawing U.S. investment will bring about positive change in South Africa.

Conversely, most opponents of disinvestment believe: (1) South Africa, with a limited, democratic government capable of peaceful change, has the potential for greater justice; (2) the volume of U.S. investment there is relatively insignificant; (3) U.S. investment does, however, support constructive change; (4) external pressure seldom brings about desired domestic policy changes; and therefore (5) withdrawing U.S. investment will have no positive effect but will be likely to affect the South African economy adversely and set back prospects for constructive change.

In this study we will examine the pronouncements of the churches on these and related issues (such as how well American firms have done in providing equal opportunity for their black employees in South Africa). We will not deal directly with the churches' views on apartheid, which is almost universally condemned. Other points to be addressed are how disinvestment would affect (1) South Africa's economic impact on its neighbors and (2) its military and strategic value to the West. Events in South Africa reverberate throughout the sub-Saharan region and affect neighboring states, such as Mozambique, Angola, and Zimbabwe. And because of South Africa's strategic significance, actions against the government may also have serious and adverse consequences in Europe, North America, and the rest of Africa.

How Large Is U.S. Investment?

The size of U.S. investment in South Africa is disputed. Even among those who agree on the *amount* of that investment, there is disagreement over its *impact*. Lawrence Litvak, Robert DeGrasse, and

Kathleen McTigue of the South Africa Catalyst Project noted in 1978 that after Britain, "America is the largest foreign investor in South Africa. . . . American companies have at least $1.665 billion of direct investments in South Africa, comprising 17 per cent of all direct foreign investments there."[26]

Philip L. Christenson, accepting essentially the same figures, emphasized that in relative terms U.S. investment is small. He wrote in 1981 that U.S. firms "account for 3 per cent of the annual capital spending in South Africa." A cutoff of new American investment, he said, "would reduce South Africa's gross domestic investment by less than 0.5 per cent."[27] Furthermore, he said, there is "no field in which an American firm operates in South Africa without other foreign and increasingly local competitors."[28]

The best estimates are that direct American investment equals 17.4 per cent of the direct foreign investment (about $2 billion) and 4 per cent of all private investment in South Africa.[29] Some activists have asserted that these figures substantially underestimate the size of U.S. investment. A report in *Multinational Monitor,* a monthly publication of Ralph Nader's Corporate Accountability Research Group, noted a "secret State Department study" that put the total amount of U.S. investment in South Africa at $14.6 billion.[30] This figure has not been corroborated by the U.S. Commerce Department or the South African government, nor is it generally accepted by economists or even disinvestment advocates. Deputy Assistant Secretary of State Frank Wisner told a congressional committee that the $14.6 billion figure is not correct "because it is not based on standard procedures of calculating investments."[31]

Assessing the impact of American investment is, of course, even harder. American firms in South Africa employ about 100,000 workers, of whom 70 per cent are black. (The labor force in South Africa is about 9.65 million.) Some analysts say that between five and six million South African blacks (workers plus their families) are dependent for their livelihoods on multinational corporations.[32] A rule of thumb is that black South African households have six members, so about 420,000 people are dependent on U.S. firms for their income.

Proponents of investment believe that as blacks make economic progress, South African social and political structures will inevitably be altered. Black advances toward greater equality during the 1970s, they say, were due largely to a booming economy. Opponents contend that foreign investors lend credibility and support to an oppressive racial regime. Chapter 5 will compare these two views of the impact of foreign investment in light of statements by the churches and the empirical evidence.

The Sullivan Principles

Many American firms operating in South Africa follow a system of equal-opportunity principles developed by Dr. Leon Sullivan, a Baptist minister from Philadelphia who also sits on the board of directors of General Motors. In 1974, after long involvement in the U.S. civil-rights movement, Sullivan proposed a code of conduct to guide U.S. firms in their employment practices in South Africa. His frequent meetings with high-level management of several U.S. companies resulted in the "Sullivan Code of Conduct," or "Sullivan Principles," promulgated in March 1977. Its six basic principles are:

1. Desegregation in work facilities, including cafeterias and lavatories.

2. Equal pay for comparable work.

3. Equal and fair employment practices, including hiring, firing, and advancement criteria.

4. Training programs to prepare non-whites for supervisory, administrative, technical, and clerical jobs.

5. Recruitment of qualified non-whites for management and supervisory positions.

6. Improvement of the living conditions—housing, transportation, education, recreation, and medical care—of non-white workers.

(A fuller statement of the code is found in appendix B.)

Initially, twelve U.S. firms agreed to observe the Sullivan Principles. Within two years the number had risen to ninety-eight. By 1982, 150 U.S. corporations and subsidiaries had signed the code, but the number had fallen to 128 by January 1983. (A signatory firm must pay dues to the Sullivan oversight committee and a fee to the Arthur D. Little Company to evaluate the firm's conduct. Firms that do not make the payments are dropped from the official list.) Over 150 other U.S. firms with business in South Africa, mostly small ones—for example, the *New York Times* and the *Washington Post*—have not signed. A complete list of Sullivan signatories is found in appendix C.

The adherence of many U.S. firms to the Sullivan Principles, coupled with pressures from within the country, has led many South

African firms to adopt similar codes. The Urban Foundation and the Employers Consultative Committee on Labour Affairs are among the South African organizations that have helped to implement labor codes.

RELIGIOUS AND ETHICAL PRINCIPLES

Improvement in the status of blacks in South Africa is a political, economic, and moral imperative. The churches and individual believers as citizens must confront alternative ways of bringing about fuller respect for human dignity. Traditionally, the churches have held that revolution is justified only in a society unable to end tyranny by legal or peaceful means. This view is akin to the doctrine of the just war, which provides a set of conditions informed by theological, philosophical, and common-sense principles designed to restrain warmaking, such as, Is there a just cause? Is there right intention? Is there a reasonable chance of success? Ernest W. Lefever has summarized Abraham Lincoln's framing of the ethical problem: People have a right to overthrow a tyrannical or utterly corrupt ruler or government when three conditions are met. First, they must have suffered the tyrant for some time; second, they must have exhausted all legal and peaceful means of getting rid of him; and third, the prospect for the tyrant's disappearing without their intervention must be bleak. Under those conditions, said Lincoln, the people have not only a right but an obligation to remove the tyrant, by violent means if necessary.[33]

In the Middle Ages the church would sometimes grant legitimacy to revolution, but such justification could be granted only *after* the fact. No theological principles could be invoked to encourage or incite revolution. This position has survived most clearly in the Roman Catholic Church, but it also exists in modified forms in the Lutheran, Calvinist, and Anglican traditions.

The Reverend Allan Boesak explained the problem in contemporary terms: "The task of the church is to work as hard as it possibly can to use non-violent means to change the situation." The church, he said, must persuade people to turn away from the option of taking up weapons and toward the option of peaceful negotiation. "Sanctification of violence does not exist. Justification of it does not exist," although the church can understand why some oppressed people who feel helpless and powerless might "become so desperate that the taking up of the gun is the only answer."[34]

This desperation explains in part the emergence of the school of doctrine and action known as "liberation theology."[35] In it, spiritual redemption is identified with political and social liberation in this world. Liberation theologians often invoke the story of the Exodus in the Bible—Israel's redemption from slavery is their model for freeing all poor and oppressed people from the bondage of their political or economic systems.[36] Moderate liberation theologians require only a constructive engagement with society to effect change while the more radical liberationists demand political, systemic, even violent revolution to purge society of its faults. Liberation theology was developed initially in a Latin American setting, but its basic ideas have been adapted to conditions in Africa and Asia as well.

In the next three chapters we will summarize and evaluate statements and pronouncements by the World Council of Churches, the South African churches, and American religious groups. We may assume that the church bodies and their leaders all share a desire for peace, freedom, and justice in South Africa. Their concern is grounded in traditional Christian compassion and a concern for the commonweal. There is little disagreement on ultimate ends; the debate is over means.

In examining these position statements, we should bear in mind the following questions: (1) Are ends, means, and consequences all given due weight? Are short-term goals sacrificed for long-term objectives or vice versa? Are immediate and harmful results overlooked because the focus is on distant and perhaps visionary goals? (2) Are the pronouncements true to the religious tradition they speak for? Or are the historical perspective and political analysis more closely aligned with some secular system of analysis and prescription, such as Marxism or democratic capitalism? (3) Do the pronouncements acknowledge the existence and validity of other points of view? Do policy suggestions grant flexibility and maneuverability to policy-makers, whether in government or in business? (4) Finally, do the pronouncements reflect intellectual integrity? Do they invoke empirical evidence to support their conclusions? Do they take into account all relevant circumstances—economic, political, diplomatic—that may impinge upon the proposed strategies for change?

CHAPTER TWO

The World Council of Churches: 'Isolating Apartheid'

THE WORLD COUNCIL OF CHURCHES was established in 1948 to provide a forum for Christian churches and to express greater Christian unity in three areas: doctrine, evangelization, and social witness. It is not a "superchurch" but rather an association of denominations; since its founding, it has grown from 152 member churches in 46 countries to 295 member churches in 100 countries. The WCC claims to represent 400 million Christians worldwide.

Not all churches belong to the Council, but it has many Protestant and Orthodox members, including the Russian Orthodox Church. The most conspicuous non-member is the Roman Catholic Church. Also outside are some large American Protestant churches, including the Southern Baptist Convention, the Lutheran Church–Missouri Synod, and several black denominations. Many evangelical and fundamentalist communions have not joined. Most South African churches are not WCC members; none of the influential Dutch Reformed churches is.

As part of its social witness, the WCC addresses many political issues. It has dealt extensively with questions of war and peace, liberation and revolution, poverty and hunger. Its public pronouncements on these matters have been criticized, especially in recent years, for being unrepresentative of the views of the majority of men and women in the pews of its constituent churches.[1] This is not necessarily a fault. Many member denominations are governed not by democratically elected bodies but by more traditional hierarchies. It would not be fair or useful to demand that the WCC, a non-political, nongovernmental organization, adhere to strictly democratic standards of representation.

The WCC's most authoritative policy-making body is the Assembly, which generally meets every seven years. The Assembly has met in Amsterdam, the Netherlands (1948); Evanston, Illinois (1954); New Delhi, India (1961); Uppsala, Sweden (1968); Nairobi, Kenya (1975); and Vancouver, British Columbia (1983). Between Assemblies, decisions are made by the 135-member Central Committee, which has an Executive Committee; both are chaired by the Secretary General. The headquarters staff that initiates, formulates, and implements policy is located in Geneva, Switzerland.

The WCC constitution does not permit the Council to exercise authority over its constituent bodies. Each member body has the right to ratify, amend, or reject the WCC's pronouncements and actions. Several, notably the Presbyterian Church in Ireland and the Salvation Army, have strenuously opposed some of the World Council's political activities—especially its financial aid to guerrilla organizations—and have suspended their membership.[2]

In the public eye, the social concerns and political activities of the WCC appear to have overwhelmed its theological and spiritual ministry. Controversies over the Council's aid to guerrillas in Namibia and Rhodesia in the 1970s tended to dominate media coverage of WCC activities. Its heavy attention to political issues has dismayed some constituent bodies, particularly those in the Eastern Orthodox tradition.

The Council has been particularly vocal and active in its concerns about southern Africa. It has been influential in the worldwide campaign against apartheid. A former South African information secretary said the WCC helped promote the idea that "the faster a crisis develops in the South African economy, the faster a change of power would occur in favor of the black population."[3]

PROGRAM TO COMBAT RACISM

The World Council has been concerned about racism since its founding. The first Assembly in 1948 said: "We protest discrimination or segregation on the grounds of race or color."[4] Six years later, at the Evanston Assembly, the delegates were more adamant: "Racial and ethnic fears, hates, and prejudices are more than social problems. . . . They are sins against God and his commandments."[5] This stance on racism was connected to the WCC's sympathy for those seeking to end colonialism in the Third World, particularly in Africa.

The New Delhi Assembly in 1961 set an important precedent for WCC attitudes toward revolutionary movements by passing (179 to 177) a resolution placing the WCC firmly on the side of those groups in Angola struggling against the Portuguese colonial government. Votes against the resolution came primarily from those concerned about singling out one country for condemnation. In another action the Assembly was more conciliatory; its "Message to Christians in South Africa" said: "Racial strife is a world problem, and we stand behind the convictions on this matter expressed by the Evanston Assembly in 1954. . . . May dignity and unity among men be established through the righteousness of God, in your land as well as those from which we come."[6]

The fourth Assembly, at Uppsala, Sweden, in 1968, reaffirmed the moderate tone of the New Delhi message but called for a "vigorous campaign" against racism around the world. South Africa was not mentioned by name in any resolutions. The Assembly resolved that the Church "must confront individuals who hold racial prejudices with the truth about our common humanity and emphasize the personal worth of all men." The message was one of improving communication: to end racial divisions and political tensions, Christians must "seek to open and keep open the lines of communication between the races, age-groups, nations, and blocs." The Uppsala Assembly also re-affirmed a declaration of the first Assembly in 1948 that "war as a method of settling disputes is incompatible with the teachings and example of our Lord Jesus."[7]

In 1969, the WCC Central Committee endorsed the recommendations of a WCC-sponsored conference held at Notting Hill, England, which asserted that churches should take a strong position in favor of "liberation groups" actively engaged in armed struggle against colonial and racist governments. This was meant to include both moral and material support. Member churches from South Africa voiced strong opposition to this view. The South African Council of Churches said: "We are disturbed by the way in which churches and the World Council . . . are called upon to initiate the use of means usually associated with the civil power in the struggle against racism. These are the weapons of the world rather than of the Church."[8]

The PCR 'Special Fund'

To implement the Notting Hill principles, the WCC launched a Program to Combat Racism (PCR) in January 1970. The most controversial aspect of this program was the "Special Fund" set up at the September 1970 annual meeting of the Central Committee to aid organizations fighting racism. Six criteria were established. The grants were (1) "to be used for humanitarian activities"; (2) to be given to groups that "combat racism," not to welfare organizations eligible for aid from other WCC departments; (3) to focus "on raising the level of awareness and on strengthening the organizational capabilities of the racially oppressed people"; (4) to be "made without control over the manner in which they are spent"; (5) to give priority to southern Africa because of "the overt and intensive nature of white racism" there; and (6) to produce maximum effect: "token grants" were not to be made unless they might lead to greater contributions from other sources.[9]

The Executive Committee reaffirmed these criteria at its 1971 meeting, citing the Uppsala Assembly's call to the Council to "embark on a vigorous campaign against racism" and to begin a "crash program to guide the Council and member churches in the urgent matter of racism."

When setting up the PCR Special Fund, the Central Committee appropriated $200,000 and asked member churches to contribute an additional $300,000. It is not clear whether all of the $300,000 was specifically directed to the Fund by the member churches or whether some was diverted from general funds given to the WCC. The Fund also accepts donations from individuals and organizations, non-member churches, and governments, with the stipulation that government support not exceed 50 per cent of the total. Contributions have come primarily from churches in Western Europe and America but also from the governments of Norway, Sweden, and the Netherlands and from the East German organization "Bread for the World."[10]

Critics soon pointed out the absence of guarantees that the grants to so-called national liberation forces would not be used for guerrilla war activities, subversion, and terrorism. The WCC staff replied that the money would be used exclusively for "educational and humanitarian work." But even if that were so, countered one critic, the Inter-Church

Relations Board of the Presbyterian Church in Ireland, "grants made by well-intentioned donors to paramilitary or guerrilla groups . . . do not end simply with humanitarian aid" but strengthen the overall operation of the receiving groups by freeing other funds for guerrilla activities.[11]

Groups Receiving Grants

From 1970 to 1980, the Program to Combat Racism gave substantial amounts to three guerrilla organizations fighting the South African government: the South West African People's Organization (SWAPO), $698,500; the African National Congress (ANC), $295,000; and the Pan Africanist Congress (PAC), $162,000. These organizations have claimed responsibility for numerous terrorist attacks since the early 1960s. The ANC, for instance, took credit for a May 1983 bombing in Pretoria that killed nineteen bystanders, all civilians. In addition, the Program gave smaller grants to two other South African groups, the Lutuli Memorial Foundation of the ANC ($32,500 over four years) and the South African Congress of Trade Unions ($20,000 over four years). The total was more than half the aid given by the PCR to all organizations in Africa during that decade and over a quarter of the aid it gave worldwide.[12]

SWAPO, the ANC, and the PAC were each waging a terrorist campaign against South Africa with the political direction and material assistance of the Soviet Union. (Their ties to the South African Communist Party have been well documented.[13]) Both the ANC and the PAC had been banned after the Sharpeville tragedy of 1960, when police opened fire on demonstrators at a PAC protest, killing about seventy civilians; many were shot in the back and were apparently fleeing the site, not advancing against the police. Since then the groups have operated from bases outside South Africa with logistical, financial, and political support from other African "liberation" groups, some African governments, the Soviet Union, and the People's Republic of China. In 1984 the WCC Special Fund gave $70,000 to the ANC to "unite and lead the oppressed people of South Africa," $30,000 to the PAC, and $100,000 to SWAPO for legal aid and "publicity and information work."[14]

In 1973 the South African Council of Churches sent a delegation to the WCC Central Committee to express its concerns about the policy of giving funds to avowedly revolutionary groups. In its message the

South African body rejected "violence and terror in all forms as a means to bring about political change" and reiterated "a commitment to combat racism, injustice, and oppression by all means consistent with the Gospel."[15]

In addition to the grants to revolutionary/liberation movements seeking to overthrow the South African regime, many other grants made through the Program to Combat Racism from 1970 to 1980 in Europe, America, and elsewhere went to organizations dealing primarily or solely with South African affairs. In Japan, both the Anti-Apartheid Committee and the Anti-Apartheid Movement received grants. In Australia, $25,000 went to the Southern Africa Liberation Centre; in New Zealand, $21,500 over four years to the National Anti-Apartheid Committee. The only group in Austria to get a grant was the Anti-Apartheid Movement ($3,000 in 1980); an identically named group in Switzerland was the only Swiss recipient of PCR funds ($16,000 over four years). In France, Britain, the Netherlands, West Germany, and Belgium, anti-apartheid groups received the bulk of the World Council's PCR grants.

The figures for 1970-80 were: Groups actively opposing the South African government—notably the African National Congress, the Pan-Africanist Congress, and SWAPO—received 59 per cent of all PCR funds distributed in Africa, and 29 per cent of the worldwide contributions. In Europe, anti-apartheid activist groups received 25 per cent of PCR grants; in Asia, similar groups got 24 per cent. Altogether, 37 per cent of PCR funds have gone to specifically anti-apartheid organizations.

In 1982, Baldwin Sjollema, director of the Program to Combat Racism from 1970 to 1981, evaluated the Special Fund's success. Its grants to organizations in southern Africa, he said, "have enabled the WCC to be in a better position to interpret the struggles for liberation in Southern Africa from the perspective of the people engaged in the struggle. They have been of considerable political significance to the racially oppressed people of Southern Africa and especially to the liberation movements."[16]

This review of the WCC's support of groups opposing the racial policies of South Africa is a necessary backdrop for understanding the Council's strong position against external investment in that country. Both strategies are designed to bring down the present Pretoria regime.

THE DISINVESTMENT STRATEGY

In *The World Council of Churches and Bank Loans to South Africa,* a 1977 book, the staff of the Program to Combat Racism reiterated the philosophical underpinnings of the WCC's strategy to discourage investment in South Africa:

> The World Council of Churches has learned that action with a specific and well-defined focus usually stands a far better chance of achieving its aims than action which is general and unspecific. White South Africa is bound to be a focus for the concerns of the WCC, not least because it seeks to explain its ideology and its behavior in terms of its vision of Christian civilization. This vision draws succor from the sterilities of Afrikaner Calvinism, which has so far perverted the Christian revelation as to cite it in support of its repugnant doctrines of racial separation. There is no way in which the WCC could avoid giving the highest priority to South Africa. . . .
>
> No one now doubts, least of all the South Africans themselves, that money from the rest of the world is vital to the maintenance of the present policies of the South African Government, and to the system of apartheid which is their cornerstone. White South Africa depends for its continued way of life on foreigners' money.[17]

A proposal for an investment boycott had been made at the 1968 Uppsala Assembly, but the delegates did not endorse it. In 1972 the Central Committee, meeting in Utrecht, decided to begin a disinvestment campaign. After a ten-day deliberation the committee urged foreign corporations to withdraw investments and operations from South Africa, South West Africa (now called Namibia), Rhodesia (now Zimbabwe), and Portuguese-controlled Angola, Mozambique, and Guinea (now Guinea-Bissau) because they had racist, colonialist governments that oppressed their non-white populations. The program, known as the Utrecht Disinvestment Strategy, was described in a 1973 PCR book called *Time to Withdraw: Investments in Southern Africa.* It urged "all member churches, Christian agencies, and individual Christians outside Southern Africa to use all their influence . . . to press corporations to withdraw investments from and cease trading with these countries."[18] Nearly 1,000 corporations were identified as targets.

In asserting that "withdrawal of foreign capital is a morally and politically sound position," the PCR argued that "the contribution of foreign capital and expertise to white South Africa's ability to consolidate its control is crucial and outweighs small gains to a few blacks who may benefit from employment in foreign-owned companies."[19] Therefore, it was argued, "the only legitimate demand possible by those wishing to challenge that control is that the companies withdraw from South Africa."[20]

In 1974 the Central Committee met in West Berlin and instructed its Finance Committee to solicit assurances from several European banks that they would cease making loans to the South African government. These banks included the Deutsche Bank (West Germany), Société Générale (France), Amsterdam-Rotterdam Bank, N.V., Société Générale de Banques S.A. (Belgium), and Creditanstalt-Bankverein (Austria). It also urged all member churches to "use their influence to press" these and other banks throughout the world "to cease granting loans to the South African government and its agencies."[21]

In a "Resolution on Comprehensive Sanctions Against South Africa" passed in Geneva in 1980,[22] the Central Committee urged the WCC and its member churches to declare apartheid a sin that must be rejected as a "perversion of the Christian gospel." It asked the churches to encourage and support the activities of the South African Council of Churches and to express solidarity "with all those in that country who struggle for a more just society." It condemned the South African government's homelands policy and "the consequent artificial creation of an urban/rural division of the black population and the use of a black middle class as a buffer." It also called for increased pressure on South Africa from abroad:

> [The churches should] press governments and international organizations to enforce comprehensive sanctions against South Africa, including a withdrawal of investments, an end to bank loans, arms embargo and oil sanctions and in general for the isolation of the state of South Africa; [and] cease any direct, and as far as possible indirect, financial involvement in activities which support the apartheid regime.[23]

In addition to supporting economic and cultural sanctions, the WCC World Consultation on Racism in 1980 urged Christian churches to "reject dialogue and relations with the Dutch Reformed Church as long as it does not allow the presence and active participation of authentic spokespersons of the oppressed people of South Africa."[24]

In his 1982 book *Isolating Apartheid*, former PCR director Baldwin Sjollema made a number of recommendations for World Council policies toward South Africa during the 1980s, basing them in part on the 1980 Central Committee decisions. He urged churches and religious agencies to work toward (among other things) "unilateral or multi-lateral government action aiming at an oil boycott against South Africa," "a refusal to import South African coal," and "an end to all export credit guarantees to South Africa." He also called for "an end to landing rights" for South African Airways abroad and an end to "cultural agreements and exchange programs with South Africa."[25]

Sjollema's final recommendation was that Christians regularly publish "well-researched documentation" in order to "help the public better understand the true nature of the struggle." This would "counter the increasingly strong and relentless propaganda of the apartheid regime and its lobbies in many parts of the world."[26]

1983 VANCOUVER ASSEMBLY ACTIONS

In keynote addresses to the 1983 WCC Assembly in Vancouver, British Columbia, German theologians Dorothee Sölle and Ulrich Duchrow asserted that apartheid was evidence of worldwide economic injustice. Sölle argued that the downtrodden throughout the world suffer from it: "Apartheid is not just a political system in an African country; apartheid is a certain way of thinking, feeling, and living without being conscious of what is happening around us. There is a way of doing theology in which the poor and economically exploited are never seen or heard—and that is apartheid theology."[27]

Duchrow said that apartheid demonstrates the inequities of the world economic system:

> My question is whether apartheid is not just the tip of an iceberg. We inhabitants of the industrialized nations, together with a few small elites in the countries of Asia, Africa and Latin America, exploit the majority of the world's population just as systemat-ically as the white South Africans do the majority of the people in South Africa. The demon of profit for the few at the expense of the many, i.e. their impoverishment, has the whole world economic system firmly in its grip, with all the side-effects of this in the form of discrimination and the suppression of human rights.[28]

Christians, he said, by their words and actions must "dissociate them-selves clearly . . . from such a system, either at specific points or even completely."[29]

In response to these exhortations, the Assembly passed a resolution on southern Africa that condemned South Africa's new constitutional proposals and its homelands policy (both discussed in chapter 1), South African military actions in Namibia and Angola, and the Reagan administration's policy of "constructive engagement" with southern Africa.

The Assembly then renewed the World Council's call to member churches for "disengagement from those institutions economically engaged in South Africa." It affirmed the need for "mandatory and comprehensive sanctions" against the country, and urged governments to stop the use of their countries' vessels for carrying oil to South Africa, "to bring an effective halt to the fueling of apartheid."[30]

EVALUATION OF WCC ACTIVITIES

Two elements underlie WCC actions on South Africa: (1) a legitimate theological, ethical, political, and social concern about apartheid and derogations of human rights, and (2) a belief that the best way to eliminate apartheid is to support revolutionary and even terrorist activities to overthrow the government in Pretoria and replace it by a "majority" non-white regime of blacks, coloreds, and Asians. These revolutionary activities must be aided through economic sanctions, including boycotts and disinvestment.

The WCC rejects the path of evolutionary change and reform. Its views are identical to those of Bishop Desmond Tutu, general secretary of the South African Council of Churches, who in 1981 called all reform "merely cosmetic and superficial."[31] He also said: "The appearance of change is a government attempt to hoodwink the international community. There is a crisis approaching in South Africa. The call is 'please act now for tomorrow will be too late.' Act now. Apply pressure, political, diplomatic, but above all economic, to persuade them that all interests would be best served by negotiation."[32]

Most Christians would welcome the economic advancement of blacks in South Africa, or poor people anywhere. Not so the WCC. Baldwin Sjollema wrote in 1982 that one policy of the South African government is to create "a small black middle class entitled to certain privileges because of the role they are allowed to play within the existing system. This creates in them sufficient self-interest to defend the status quo."[33] In 1980, the WCC Central Committee asked churches to condemn "the use of a black middle class as a buffer," presumably against change. WCC leaders refuse to recognize the growth of a black middle class as a major positive development, a necessary economic element in the gradual transition to a more just society. They view it instead as undesirable, because it postpones the revolutionary crisis that they regard as both inevitable and morally necessary. Ecumenical spokesmen also tend to see the development of a black middle class as evidence of the "corruption" inherent in capitalism. In their 1981 book *The South African Churches in a Revolutionary Situation,* American sociologists Marjorie Hope and James Young of Wilmington College in Ohio expressed a fear that most South African blacks were "striving for the ecologically wasteful lifestyles of whites in South Africa and the United States."[34]

At its founding Assembly in 1948, the World Council of Churches proclaimed that "war as a method of settling disputes is incompatible" with the Gospel. Yet the same body now advocates revolutionary violence as a means to settle racial disputes in southern Africa. Christians believe that the eradication of racism in any form is a legitimate goal, but most of them would not agree that supporting terrorist organizations that kill innocent people is a legitimate means for reaching that end. By supporting revolutionary violence, the WCC undermines its legitimacy in the eyes of most peace-loving citizens of the United States and Europe, and such actions have generated considerable discontent among members of the Council's constituent denominations. Those who thus lose faith in the organization as a whole are cut off from its spiritual guidance and its efforts to strengthen Christian unity. And its laudable, non-political, humanitarian programs—refugee assistance, agricultural aid, support for hospitals, schools, and orphanages—are viewed with increasing suspicion as subordinate to some ulterior political goals at variance with the classical Christian ethic.

The right or obligation to speak out on political and social issues is inherent in Christian morality. Politics and ethics are inseparable. The WCC must, however, demonstrate greater fidelity to the traditional Christian ethic as it seeks greater justice in the world. It must be more discriminating in its support for groups that "combat racism" and must deny support to any that advocate violence—particularly terrorist violence in which innocent people are targets.

The WCC rejects the evolutionary approach. It repudiates the "constructive engagement" with South Africa of business, labor, and diplomacy. It rejects efforts to create economic conditions that encourage improved wages for black workers, greater fringe benefits, and higher standards of living through better health care and housing. Some black labor leaders and others who advocate reform rather than revolution have been accused of attempting to "discredit the WCC" and of being "defenders of South African apartheid."[35] WCC publications have characterized Ronald Reagan and members of his administration as "racist" and "pro-apartheid"; a 1982 Program to Combat Racism report asserted that "rarely before has racism been such a consistent component of U.S. government policy formulations."[36]

Strangely, the WCC becomes more and more entrenched in its campaign for economic sanctions and disinvestment while substantial political reforms—such as the 1983 constitution's expansion of voting rights—are occurring and the economic lot of blacks is improving.

CHAPTER THREE

Voices From the
South African Churches

THE SOUTH AFRICAN is "a religious animal," said Dutch
Reformed theologian David Bosch.[1] According to the 1980 census,
almost 84 per cent of the population claims church membership;
among whites the percentage is nearly 94.[2] Former *Christian Science
Monitor* correspondent June Goodwin said in 1982 that "theology is
the key to understanding South Africa. . . . Christianity in myriad
forms permeates the society."[3]

Christianity came to the southern tip of Africa with the Dutch and
British colonists and with American and European missionaries. Three
Dutch Reformed denominations constitute the largest Christian group
in the country, with about 3.9 million members in racially separate
bodies. Nearly half of all white South Africans belong to one of these
denominations, all of which have non-white branches also. The other
major denominations are multi-racial. Methodists are second in total
membership, Roman Catholics third, and Anglicans fourth. Nearly 30
per cent of the blacks belong to separatist, all-black denominations or
to independent fundamentalist or pentecostal denominations. These
independent churches are unrelated to denominations inside or outside
South Africa, and many are breakaways from mission churches established in the nineteenth and early twentieth centuries. South Africa's
official handbook for 1979 noted that the rise of the black independent
church movement has been "rapid and spectacular."[4] (See appendix D
for South African church membership statistics.)

South African churches have become a focal point for political
debate. Dutch Reformed theologian Allan Boesak noted that the
churches "without wanting it, have become more and more a vehicle

for the expression of the political aspirations of black people in South Africa."[5] In 1979, Alan Paton, author of *Cry, the Beloved Country* and other novels of South African life, said his country's "fragmented society" has carried over to the churches. Afrikaner (i.e., white Dutch Reformed) churches, he wrote, "identify themselves very closely with the maintenance of Afrikaner identity" in a hostile environment. Black churches identify themselves with the cause of black liberation. But "the so-called English-speaking churches [Anglican, Catholic, Congregational, Lutheran, Methodist, Presbyterian, and others]," Paton said, "with their multi-racial character, are in no such simple position as the Afrikaner and black churches."[6]

Underscoring this diversity within the churches, Methodist theologian Charles Villa-Vicencio noted that there is "no homogeneous church in South Africa, and the numerous individual churches and church groupings have been penetrated by every ideological option facing the people of this subcontinent."[7] He identified three main currents of political-religious thought: (1) conservative or reactionary movements that support strict apartheid policies; (2) moderate elements that encourage the reformist tendencies of the present National Party government led by P. W. Botha, but do not challenge the fundamental policies of separate development; and (3) "radical Christianity, epitomized in the Ottawa resolution [a strong anti-apartheid stand] of the World Alliance of Reformed Churches, the stance taken by the SACC [South African Council of Churches] since 1978 under the leadership of its general secretary, Anglican Bishop Desmond Tutu, and the liberation theology debate." Villa-Vicencio pointed out that "not all black churches affirm [the radical] position. . . . Black theology and liberation theology does provide food for the soul for some blacks, but others regard it as a foreign intrusion into the 'pure' gospel."[8]

All major denominations in South Africa have declared either apartheid or racism a sin, thereby implying the need for fundamental change. Some churches have gone so far as to declare that support for apartheid is heretical—i.e., that rejecting apartheid is a part of Christian orthodoxy. This is the Methodist, Anglican, and Lutheran position; it is shared by the South African Council of Churches, the World Alliance of Reformed Churches, and the Alliance of Black Reformed Christians in Southern Africa. The South African Catholic bishops have called apartheid "intrinsically evil." Only the Dutch Reformed churches have limited themselves to the assertion that "racism is a sin."[9]

THE DUTCH REFORMED CHURCHES

In the realm of government policy, the most influential religious body is the Dutch Reformed Church, known by its Afrikaans initials as the NGK (Nederduitse Gereformeerde Kerk). It consists of four separate synods or branches, white, colored, black, and Asian. The white NGK, the General Synod, has 1.7 million members. It is often called "the National Party at prayer": it claims the membership of 42 per cent of the white population—roughly 72 per cent of the Afrikaans-speaking whites, who provide the major support for the National Party. The white synod has more than 1,200 congregations and 1,700 ministers.[10] References to "the NGK" usually mean the white synod only. The NG Sendingkerk or NG Mission Church, the colored branch of the NGK, has 678,000 members; the NGK in Africa, the denomination's black branch, 1.1 million; and the Reformed Church, the Indian branch, about 4,000. These three non-white branches of the NGK seem to have considerable autonomy.

There are two other Dutch Reformed denominations. The conservative white Nederduitsch Hervormde Kerk (NHK) has 246,000 members plus a mission branch of 20,000 black members called the Hervormde Kerk of Southern Africa. The Gereformeerde Kerk, an ultraconservative denomination whose 128,000 members are sometimes called *doppers,* is overwhelmingly white but has some 140 non-white mission congregations.

The Dutch Reformed tradition in South Africa regards the government as an agency ordained by God. The Federal Council of the NGK declared in 1951 that the state is a divine institution, deriving its power not from popular sovereignty but from the authority of God alone. "Humanistic conceptions of titular, legal, political, or popular sovereignty have no validity," the statement said; "further, there can be no division of power between legislature, executive, and judiciary, according to Calvinist politics."[11]

John de Gruchy, professor of religious studies at the University of Cape Town, has compared the NGK's view of church and state to the relation between the church and the Roman Empire in the time of Constantine. The effect of this relationship, he argued, is that "the church upholds the authority of the state, blessing and sanctifying its policies when necessary, and in return the state protects the freedom of the church to fulfill its religious functions."[12]

The Dutch Reformed churches have taken no stand on the investment issue. Over the past two decades, however, some observers have perceived a gradual shift in the NGK's position on apartheid, a softening of the hardline adherence to the doctrine of racial separation it promoted in the 1940s and 1950s. The shift, often dismissed as irrelevant by overseas critics of the South African government, is not thus considered by domestic critics, who are aware of the vital role the NGK can and must play in bringing about peaceful change. Bishop Desmond Tutu, leader of the South African Council of Churches and one of the most outspoken opponents of apartheid, acknowledged this when he said in 1979 that there can be no peaceful reform in South Africa until the "NGK starts to fulfill its important role in the movement for change."[13]

The three non-white branches of the NGK have condemned apartheid as sin and heresy. The white NGK and the NHK were suspended from membership in the World Alliance of Reformed Churches (WARC) for their failure to do the same. Both white churches were formerly members of the World Council of Churches also, but they left it because of its demands that they integrate their church services. Neither church is now a member of any major ecumenical organization. Most other denominations shun the two churches, refusing to engage in dialogue on theological, liturgical, social, or political issues with the NGK and NHK.

The NGK and NHK have condemned *racism* as sinful, and there has always been a vocal minority of members—both lay and clergy— pressing for a full condemnation of apartheid. The churches contend that apartheid is not a racist system; they have constructed an elaborate theological defense arguing that the policy of separate development "is not in conflict with Holy Scripture."[14] In response to its suspension by the WARC, the General Assembly of the NHK wrote: "The irrefutable fact is that this policy [separate development] has greatly improved the quality of life and brought more freedom to our peoples than in many countries of the Third World, not to mention Marxist countries."[15]

At about the same time, the General Synod of the NGK declared that it did not willingly accept the suspension of its membership in the WARC, that it "rejects all racism as unscriptural and as sin," but that "race-consciousness and the love of one's own nation is not sinful."[16] Both the NGK and NHK saw the WARC decision as an expression of liberation theology, which they regarded as more politically than religiously based.

It seems clear that no support for disinvestment or other economic sanctions against apartheid is forthcoming from the white Dutch Reformed bodies. The non-white branches, however, have left the door open. Dr. Allan Boesak, one of the most prominent Reformed opponents of apartheid, argued in 1983: "Change will come about when we address that root problem of the [apartheid] system. And change will come about when we are in a position to put unprecedented pressure on it, by taking away that ideological foundation upon which the system rests. . . . You need economic pressure, you need to tell the South African government that if you don't change, something will happen."[17]

Boesak wants to challenge apartheid both by undermining the moral or theological foundations claimed for it and by exerting economic pressure on the government. Perhaps the NG Sendingkerk, colored branch of the NGK, had the idea of economic pressure in mind when in 1982 it commended this Scripture passage to the NGK: "[The Lord said]: Whenever I hold back the rain or send locusts to eat up the crops or send an epidemic on my people, if they pray to me and repent and turn away from the evil they have been doing, then I will hear them in heaven, forgive their sins, and make their land prosperous again" (II Chron. 7:13-14).[18] But neither Boesak's reference to economic pressure nor the NG Sendingkerk's message to the NGK was a call for disinvestment. At most, the two statements were warnings that such ideas might be pursued in the future.

SOUTH AFRICAN COUNCIL OF CHURCHES

The South African Council of Churches traces its origins to the General Missionary Council, founded in 1904. In 1936 the Missionary Council was absorbed by the newly formed Christian Council of South Africa, which included both black and white churches, and in 1968 the Christian Council became the South African Council of Churches (SACC). At first, its dealings with the World Council of Churches and that body's support for "liberation movements" in southern Africa were cautious. By 1978, when it chose the black Anglican bishop Desmond Tutu as its general secretary, it had begun to work more closely with the World Council. Since then it has largely accepted the WCC's social and political positions.

The SACC is composed of fifteen member churches, nine organizations, and four observer churches. Most major Protestant denominations are members; the conspicuous exceptions are the white Dutch Reformed bodies, the NGK, NHK, and Gereformeerde Kerk. The non-white branches of the NGK are SACC participants, the colored NG Sendingkerk and the (Asian) Reformed Church in Africa as observers and the black NGK in Africa as a full member. (See appendix E.)

Relations between the SACC and the South African government are strained and often adversarial. In 1981-82 the government investigated the SACC's financial affairs, probing the sources of its funding from abroad. One result of the inquiry was the conviction of John Rees, former SACC general secretary, on charges of fraud and misappropriation of funds. The South African Council of Churches is not mentioned in the 1983 and 1984 official South African yearbooks, though in each a twenty-page chapter about religion in the country sketches all major and some minor religious denominations.

Journalist David Thomas identifies the SACC members—mainly mainline Protestant denominations such as Anglican, Methodist, Presbyterian, and Lutheran—plus the Roman Catholic Church as the "SACC-bloc" churches, because they have English as their primary language and share liberal views in theology and politics.[19] These common elements date back to the nineteenth century, when English-speaking missionaries frequently advocated more liberal positions on social issues than their indigenous Dutch Reformed counterparts.

The SACC-bloc approach to church-state relations differs significantly from the Calvinist thought of the Dutch Reformed churches, which sees government as a divine agent. A succinct explanation of this view was provided by Calvin Cook of Rhodes University:

> Christians readily grant the state its proper place in maintaining order and justice, in rewarding good and punishing evil. . . . [But] the authorities ruling over men are neither omniscient nor

infallible. . . . As one such authority the state can act and order as it pleases. However, there is a point where its action contradicts the authority of the Kingdom and its command compromises the allegiance Christians owe to God alone. Then Christians are bound to obey God rather than man.[20]

The SACC and its predecessor, the Christian Council of South Africa, have long opposed apartheid and other forms of racism. In 1949, the year after the election victory of the pro-apartheid National Party, the Christian Council adopted a resolution affirming that blacks in the mainstream of South African society "should share in the responsibilities and rights of their new status"; that "the real need in South Africa is not *apartheid* but *eendrag* (i.e., unity through team-work)"; and that "every man has the right to work in that sphere in which he can make the best use of his abilities for the common good."[21]

A Firm Stand Against Apartheid

The 1949 resolution marked the first articulation of the Christian Council's principled opposition to apartheid. The next milestone in its struggle was nearly two decades later, in 1968, when the newly re-named South African Council of Churches issued "A Message to the People of South Africa."[22] The Message said in part: "There are few areas even of the private life of the individual which are untouched by the effects of the doctrine of racial separation. . . . In South Africa, everyone is expected to believe that a man's racial identity is the most important thing about him. . . . This amounts to a denial of the central statements of the Gospel. It is opposed to the Christian understanding of the nature of man and community."[23]

The Message strongly supported resistance to apartheid and said: "If we seek to reconcile Christianity with the so-called 'South African way of life,' " Christians may have an obligation to violate "some of the customs and laws of this country."[24]

When it issued the Message, the SACC was seeking ways to assume a more visible and active role in combating racism and apartheid. In collaboration with the Christian Institute, a lay ecumenical organiza-tion that was later to be banned as subversive, the SACC sponsored the Study Project on Christianity in an Apartheid Society (SPRO-CAS). Several of the studies emanating from SPRO-CAS, especially *Migrant*

Labour in South Africa by Francis Wilson (1972), have done much to bring the human costs of apartheid to the attention of South African decision-makers as well as ordinary white citizens.

Although SPRO-CAS was phased out by the end of 1973, the collaborative efforts of the SACC and the Christian Institute continued. Together they launched the Black Community Program through which they sent organizers into the black community to help foster leadership and organizational skills, to explore "black theology"—as expressed by African and black American theologians—and to encourage "black consciousness."[25]

At the 1976 SACC National Conference, its Justice and Reconciliation Division was asked to make a study of foreign investment in South Africa, in part as a response to requests by foreign churches for a statement of the SACC's views on the subject. The resulting report, presented the following year, found that foreign investment had broken down traditional barriers against non-whites in certain job areas and had moved blacks from an agrarian to an industrial economy, but had also contributed to a massive breakup of family life (by encouraging rural workers to leave their families behind and seek urban jobs) while reinforcing the segregationist status quo. The report did not reconcile its assertions of breakdown of employment barriers and reinforcement of the status quo, nor say whether it would be preferable, in order to preserve family life, not to make jobs available to poor rural blacks.

The report carried four major recommendations: (1) investments from abroad should cease unless industries accepted an obligatory code of conduct; (2) a tripartite committee representing church, industry, and commerce should be established to monitor the code; (3) churches should review their investments to ensure that they were not involved in the liquor trade, arms manufacture, or discriminatory practices; and (4) the churches should support all schemes aimed at reducing unemployment in ways that preserve human dignity.[26]

The SACC Code

The lengthy code of conduct proposed by the SACC provides for: (1) non-segregation of the races in all eating, comfort, and work facilities; (2) equal and fair employment practices for all employees; (3) equal pay, at market rates, for all employees doing equal or comparable work; (4) training programs to prepare blacks in substantial numbers for supervisory, administrative, clerical, and technical jobs; (5) an increase of blacks in management and supervisory positions; (6) improvement of the quality of employees' lives outside the work environment; (7) refusal to use migrant labor unless quarters were provided for workers' spouses; (8) reduction in the number of foreign skilled workers and their replacement with adequately trained South African blacks; (9) immediate recognition of existing trade unions; (10) encouragement of new unions; (11) introduction of labor-intensive manufacturing and distribution processes, as opposed to increasing mechanization; (12) appointment of labor advisors to open the way for multi-racial cooperation; (13) establishment of committees in various sectors of industry to share information and problem-solving techniques; (14) a voluntary self-tax on gross corporate profits, to be contributed to education for blacks; (15) support of community development projects initiated and controlled by blacks; (16) investment of a certain proportion of companies' portfolios in banking institutions that would use the invested funds solely for the benefit of blacks; (17) refusal to invest in or assist projects connected with arms manufacture.[27]

Although many critics of foreign investment in South Africa reject the claim of American businesses that they act as a liberalizing influence in South Africa, it is significant that the first six provisions of the SACC code of conduct were borrowed almost word for word from the "Sullivan Principles," the labor code developed by American business leaders. (See page 14 and appendix B.) The SACC Justice and Reconciliation Division said the Sullivan Principles were "laudable" but did not "go to the root of the South African problem." The SACC code, therefore, was intended to improve upon the Sullivan Principles.[28]

Bishop Desmond Tutu

After his 1978 election as general secretary, Anglican bishop Desmond Tutu tried to move the SACC toward greater support for some kind of disinvestment or economic boycott policy. To this end he made several highly publicized appearances abroad.

In a 1978 address to the Royal Commonwealth Society in London, Tutu charged that foreign investments and loans had been used mainly to maintain the status quo. He warned investors that when the day of liberation comes for non-whites, "we will remember who our friends were when we sought freedom."[29] Upon his return to South Africa, Tutu admitted that he had called on foreign governments to exert diplomatic, political, and economic pressure on his country, implying that as the sports boycott (which bars South African athletes from international competitions, including the Olympic Games) had brought about certain changes in South African society, so would economic sanctions.[30] The bishop's increasing militancy was not approved by all SACC members or all leaders in his own Anglican Church. Many prominent church people dissociated themselves from his stance, including his superior, Bishop Timothy Bavin of Johannesburg.[31]

In a 1979 visit to Denmark, Tutu reaffirmed his support for punitive action against his country.[32] In September of that year the SACC executive council repudiated the bishop's call for an international boycott of South African coal. Explaining his position to the Pretoria Press Club, Tutu described the proposal as "an attempt to make a sober contribution" to a solution without using violence. "People are quite happy to talk about so-called peaceful means of change" as long as they "will be ineffectual," he said. "Most whites want change as long as things remain the same, as long they can go on enjoying their privileges." For this reason, he said, "we urge the international community to exert as much political, diplomatic, and economic pressure on South Africa as possible, to persuade us to go to the conference table. I love South Africa too passionately to want to see her destroyed, and international pressure may just avert that."[33]

In a 1981 article in the *Washington Post,* Tutu wrote that "multinational corporations are not yet involved in the business of helping to destroy apartheid. They have done some good things for their employees, but all within the framework of apartheid, and really no more than what a good employer should have been doing." Rather than dismantling apartheid, he said, corporations are making it "more comfortable."[34]

At the Vancouver Assembly of the World Council of Churches in August 1983, Tutu said, "Investment in South Africa is as much a moral issue as it is an economic situation."[35] Foreign investment in South Africa can be justified, he argued, only if two conditions are met: (1) workers must be able to live with their families near their workplace (this would require corporations to join in a successful lobbying effort against such laws as the Group Areas Act, which prevent families from living together in certain cities and towns) and (2) laborers should have mobility and freedom to sell their labor wherever they choose. Unless these conditions are met, investors "are benefitting from the misery and suffering of black people."[36]

Bishop Tutu further asserted that the Sullivan Principles merely make apartheid "more acceptable, more comfortable. We do not want to make apartheid more comfortable, we want it dismembered."[37]

Tutu's statements on economics and investment embrace certain contradictions. In his 1982 book *Crying in the Wilderness,* for instance, he praises black entrepreneurship and growing consumer power but within a few pages says, "Capitalism is exploitative and I can't stand that."[38] Elaborating upon this, he says: "From my perspective Capitalism seems to give unbridled license to human cupidity, and has a morality that belongs properly to the jungle—'the survival of the fittest, the weakest to the wall, and the devil take the hindmost.' I find what I have seen of Capitalism and the free enterprise system quite morally repulsive."[39]

Desmond Tutu was awarded the Nobel Prize for Peace in 1984. Less than a month later, he became the first black Anglican bishop of Johannesburg, succeeding Bishop Timothy Bavin. On the day the Nobel was announced, he reiterated his views on investment. "What we have to say to those who invest in South Africa," he said at a New York press conference, "is that your investment is a moral as well as an economic issue."[40] The international community, he said, must "exert pressure on the South African government . . . especially economic pressure. . . . This is our very last chance for change because if that doesn't happen . . . it seems the blood bath will be inevitable."[41] The *Rand Daily Mail,* a liberal Johannesburg newspaper, congratulated Tutu on winning the Nobel Prize but said it believed he made a "major error of judgment" in encouraging disinvestment, even while he offered "the alternative of forceful dissent to people who might otherwise conclude that violence is the only solution."[42]

The SACC and the Government

An unusual meeting of the SACC's executive council with Prime Minister P. W. Botha on August 7, 1980, drew criticism from radical churchmen, who maintained that dialogue with the government was

futile, or worse. Before the meeting, Tutu said the SACC representatives would tell Botha that there "can be no real peace until meaningful changes have been introduced—in the form of political power-
sharing."[43]   In his opening statement, the prime minister told the
delegation: "We are a Christian state and are desirous of ruling according to Christian principles, and for this reason the state is attentive to
the voice of the church, since both are concerned with the welfare of
the people entrusted to their care." After the meeting, SACC delegates
reported that their concerns were taken seriously but that there was a
wide gulf between the church and the state. Tutu reportedly said the
delegates stressed that they did not naïvely believe power could be
shared overnight but that the government must commit itself to a
common citizenship for all South Africans in an undivided nation.[44]

South African journalist David Thomas summarized a change in the
SACC position in a 1982 article. The churches "have a considerable
part to play in the opposition to apartheid," he said, because of their
extensive overseas connections, "significant in light of the fact that
church bodies overseas increasingly see their one hope of influencing
the situation in South Africa as advocating trade sanctions and disinvestment."

A decade before, said Thomas, "the official policy of the SACC was
anti-disinvestment, the organization then taking the classic liberal
position that investment and economic growth were likely to help
undermine apartheid." Since coming under the leadership of black
churchmen, the SACC had begun to take a different approach, he said,
one that "can only strengthen the hand of the divestment lobby in the
West."[45]

OTHER CHURCH STATEMENTS

Some SACC member denominations have undertaken their own studies
of the disinvestment issue. One was the **Church of the Province of
South Africa,** the Anglican body to which Bishop Tutu belongs. In
1976, under pressure from Anglicans abroad, a church committee
requested that Archbishop Bill Burnett initiate an inquiry. A commission was established, met three times, and issued its findings in
November 1977.

The report stressed that there was no perfect solution to the problem,
acknowledged the diversity of opinion on the topic, and said the 1977

SACC report on investment was "vague" and "superficial." It noted a socialist, anti-capitalist bias permeating much Western Christian social analysis of the South African situation.

The report said that foreign investment had helped to stimulate economic growth and that blacks had made significant economic strides as a result. Government policies on education, job training, and wage policy had been altered so that racial inequality in the marketplace was gradually being ameliorated. The bargaining power of the non-white community was growing through increased prosperity and changes in the class structure.

The Anglican commission urged foreign corporations to continue enlightened labor policies, concentrating on improving black living conditions and on providing job training and educational facilities. It advocated the establishment of black trade unions. The commission concluded that blacks wanted job opportunities, not revolution. The disinvestment forces, by depressing the growth rate of South Africa's economy, were playing into the hands of the "protagonists of violence," it said. Noting the emergence of a black middle class, it expressed the belief that the "creation of such a middle class is of great importance."[46]

The **Methodist Church of Southern Africa,** with 2.1 million members—including 1.5 million blacks—explained in 1981 why it had taken no position on disinvestment. Methodists in South Africa hold widely divergent views on the issue, said the church, and "every person has the moral and Christian right to hold and express such views and the duty to hear and seriously consider the views of those who differ."[47]

Of the major Christian denominations, the **Roman Catholic Church** is the fastest growing among South Africa's blacks. In 1980 it had 1.7 million black members, 400,000 whites, 260,000 coloreds, and 21,000 Asians.[48]

The Catholic Church has always actively opposed apartheid, and in 1976 it began admitting black students to previously all-white schools in defiance of the law. Although the government initially ignored the action, in 1977 provincial administrators in Transvaal and Cape Province ordered the Catholic schools to expel the black students. The Catholic bishops refused and were assured of support by the Vatican. The government has since not enforced its segregation orders. Also in

1977, the Southern African Catholic Bishops' Conference expressed its conviction, "so often repeated, that the only solution to our racial tensions consists in conceding full citizen and human rights to all persons in the republic."

The Catholic hierarchy has taken no position on disinvestment,[49] but in 1980 the Bishops' Conference published a paper by a group called Young Christian Workers that addressed the church's traditional concern for employer-employee relations. The paper examined wage and working conditions, criticized the job-reservation system, called for full recognition of black trade unions and for greater job training for non-whites, and pointed out the responsibilities of both workers and employers. It also related "investment" to exploitation: "We urge all Christians, religious organizations, institutions, and parishes to query how their money is being invested and to what extent they are indirectly maintaining exploitation. Further, we urge them to investigate the possibilities of using their influence, however limited, to hamper investments in firms maintaining exploitation."[50]

On visits to the United States, individual South African bishops have expressed their support for external investment. Archbishop Joseph P. Fitzgerald of Johannesburg said in 1981 that the anti-apartheid movement would suffer a setback if American corporations were to divest themselves of their South African holdings. Such actions, he argued, would hold back the development of the non-white economic base.[51]

Archbishop Denis E. Hurley of Durban argued in 1982 that business was turning against apartheid. As the economy becomes more industrialized, he said, "the practice is growing in industry to accept blacks" in higher-level jobs, and "industry is becoming an opponent to apartheid because it can't get trained personnel." Archbishop Hurley, then president of the Bishops' Conference, said he was unsure whether economic sanctions against South Africa would ultimately help or hurt the struggle for justice.[52]

The **Christian Institute of Southern Africa** was formed after the Cottesloe Conference of December 1960, at which representatives of the World Council of Churches met South African church leaders to discuss the race situation. The aim of the interracial and ecumenical institute was to promote peace, "but not [the] peace of avoiding conflict."[53] Its leader was the Reverend C. F. Beyers Naudé, a prominent NGK clergyman whose participation in the Christian Institute led to social ostracism and eventual "banning" by the South African government in 1977. (The banning order, under which Naudé was forbidden to speak in public, meet with more than two other persons at the same time, or be quoted in the media, was lifted in 1984.) Under Naudé's leadership, the Christian Institute openly supported black revolutionary/liberation movements. In 1976, it declared its support for an investment boycott. Essentially it acquiesced to the presence of existing investments but argued that there should be no further investment because "strong economic pressure is of vital importance in bringing about as peaceful a solution as possible" and because "investment in South Africa is investment in apartheid, and thus immoral, unjust, and exploitative."[54] The institute argued that attempts to improve the situation through "pressure by investors have proved inadequate" and that the argument that "economic growth can produce fundamental change" was false.[55]

The declaration went on, however, to ask investors with funds already in South Africa to behave more humanely, to improve relations between workers and management, to improve black training and job advancement, and to promote stable family life for their employees.[56]

The **Baptist Union of Southern Africa,** a 60,000-member, multiracial denomination, has not made a formal pronouncement on disinvestment, but its general secretary, the Reverend Trevor M. Swart, has said that "if any consideration were given to disinvestment in this country, the people you are trying to help most would be hurt most."[57]

The **Full Gospel Church of God** is a multi-ethnic pentecostal denomination with 605 black, 193 white, 138 Asian, and 70 colored churches. Its moderator, Pastor M. L. Badenhorst, wrote in early 1983 of his denomination's opposition to disinvestment strategies:

> A policy of consultation and co-operation has proved to be far more effective than all the boycott threats and actions of the past. You do not promote an attitude of change when you take the bread out of a man's mouth. When you befriend him and reason with him you can surely influence a reasonable person. I would, therefore, say that the present American policy towards South Africa is far more productive and fruitful than previous policies. I believe large American companies with strong South African investments have accepted a policy of assisting the less privileged members of the South African society by paying them better wages and creating better working conditions for them. This is commendable and I believe this should be encouraged.[58]

Pastor Badenhorst added that disinvestment "would harm the South African economy, and the first people and most of the people to be hurt would be the non-white communities. In our thinking the strategy of this action would . . . cause large-scale unemployment and suffering among the less privileged communities in the hope that this will stir up political riots and revolution."[59]

The **Church of England in South Africa,** a 72,000-member multi-racial denomination (not to be confused with the Church of the Province of South Africa, another Anglican body), declared in a 1979 statement that while it deplored "every kind of injustice, all racism and all discrimination on the grounds of color," the church deplored "equally the violence of terrorists which the WCC and the SACC seem to condone." The statement criticized the two ecumenical bodies for venturing into the realm of politics, "thereby giving an impression to the world at large that the Church is merely another political party or pressure group, willing to use force, violence, and anarchy to achieve its aims."[60]

Church registrar Herbert Hammond, the denominational official charged with recording church positions on social and theological issues, said that the church, whose competence is "in matters appertaining to God and pointing men and women to an understanding of his mind and purpose," moved outside its realm when issuing opinions on disinvestment. "Would the church ask for the advice of the president of an American corporation or the U.S. government for that matter in the conduct of its affairs? To pose that question is also to answer it."[61]

The **Apostolic Church (Apostle Unity)** has not formally spoken on disinvestment, but church moderator J. P. Erasmus wrote in 1983 that the church's "official viewpoint" is against it, because disinvestment "would be detrimental to the very people it is designed to help." It would probably also be ineffective in influencing the government; disinvestment "could perhaps harm the economy in the short term, but adjustments and other measures would be introduced. The investors themselves would suffer most."[62] Erasmus added that "the government and the people are more than able to solve the problems which in our multinational state are rather complex without outside interference."[63]

The Spiritual Committee of the 30,000-member, multi-racial **Maranatha Pentecostal Church** issued a statement in early 1983 supporting external investment because "the blacks, colored, and some whites will benefit as work opportunities would [increase]. . . . If American and other national corporations or firms should withdraw their investments in South Africa, the severity of suffering would be on the side of the blacks and coloreds."[64]

South Africa's small community of religious **Jews** has not issued any formal pronouncements on investment, but Rabbi E. J. Duschinsky, head of the Jewish Ecclesiastical Court in Cape Province, pointed out that there are "strong feelings in the Jewish and specially in the Moslem leadership—both minority denominations—that such actions might, in the first place, hurt the underprivileged masses of non-white population groups and rather than being a long-range leader to the ultimate alleviation of their plight, might be, if protracted, a source of additional suffering, destitution, and despair." He added: "In the view of the Jewish religious leadership as I know it, disinvestment, or boycott, is a militant economic weapon, while our religious leadership demands of us the pursuit of pacification, welfare, peace, and happiness."[65]

EVALUATION OF CHURCH VIEWS

Americans who pass judgment on South African affairs too often do so without adequate information, particularly about the effects their proposals would have on the South Africans they are trying to help. Herbert Hammond, registrar of the Church of England in South Africa, compared the disinvestment issue to an American controversy: "To a citizen of another country, such as myself, it became very difficult to understand what the turmoil in the United States on the issue of Vietnam was all about. It just depended on whom one read last."[66]

A brief survey of pronouncements by South African churches does not do justice to the complexity of the issues that these churches face. Investment is only one aspect of the theological, political, and social problems the churches must address. The best study of church attitudes toward apartheid is John W. de Gruchy's *The Church Struggle in South Africa* (1979), which explores not only the resistance to apartheid by the so-called English-speaking churches but also the justification given it by the Dutch Reformed denominations and their modifications of that position.

With this in mind, it is difficult to generalize from the evidence presented here about the views of South African churches on investment. Since opinion is divided and no significant survey research is available, it is not possible to assert that South African church leaders are "for" or "against" disinvestment or other economic sanctions. What follows is an impressionistic interpretation of evidence gathered largely from church leaders who may or may not accurately reflect the views of the members of their denominations.

With the exception of leaders of the South African Council of Churches, notably Bishop Tutu, and independent groups such as the Christian Institute, most church leaders in South Africa appear to support continued economic investment from abroad and thus to be against disinvestment. They encourage businesses to treat their employees fairly, following the Sullivan Principles or the SACC code. Many insist that disinvestment would hurt most the very people it is intended to help. Some express grave doubts over the efficacy of an externally imposed disinvestment strategy, and others have registered their concern over the World Council of Churches' support of violent liberation movements in southern Africa and elsewhere.

In addition, some church leaders, especially in independent Protestant denominations, find the attitude of American and other foreign proponents of disinvestment rather arrogant. They insist that advocating an investment boycott constitutes unconscionable and detrimental interference in the internal affairs of another country. South Africa's problems, they say, are for South Africans, not outsiders, to solve.[67]

CHAPTER FOUR

American Churches Speak Out

IN SEPTEMBER 1981, Donald McHenry, former U.S. ambassador to the United Nations, chaired an unusual meeting of 125 church activists and corporate executives at the International House in New York City. The occasion was a "Symposium on Current Issues Facing American Corporations in South Africa." It grew out of a dialogue between church leaders and the management of Ford and General Motors and consisted of three panel discussions: the performance of U.S. corporations in the workplace, U.S. companies and the South African government, and how corporations can contribute to constructive social change in South Africa.

The diversity of views expressed by religious leaders at this meeting reflected the diversity that exists in American churches over the investment issue. Pronouncements by American churches, church leaders, and ecumenical organizations range from strident support for disinvestment (National Council of Churches) to neutrality (National Conference of Catholic Bishops) to pragmatic rejection (United Church of Christ). Many other church groups maintain anti-investment positions, varying in tone and comprehensiveness. Still others do not oppose investment in South Africa or do not consider it an issue appropriate for official pronouncements.

Twenty-nine banks and other companies doing business in South Africa were represented at the International House discussions, along with thirty churches and religious communities. Church activists at the meeting maintained that South Africa is not moving quickly enough to redress black grievances. United Presbyterian executive William Thompson asserted: "There have been no meaningful social or political changes in South Africa."[1] Laws restricting black trade unions and mandating the resettling of blacks, some church representatives argued, blunted the commendable efforts of U.S. corporations to improve the lot of their black workers. Unless far-reaching changes occur in the country, said Avery Post, president of the United Church of Christ, "the good we try to do can be coopted by the powers of evil."[2] Some church activists also said that U.S. corporations were contributing to the support of apartheid. Sister Regina Murphy of the Sisters of Charity charged that "the record shows a comfortable commercial relationship in which many U.S. companies have sold strategic products and technological skills to assist the South African government in its apartheid policy."[3]

In contrast, David Preus, presiding bishop of the American Lutheran Church, supported continued investment as a means of contributing to the "erosion" of the apartheid system.[4] "Without directly entering the political process," he said, "corporate executives can, in personal dialogue, implant and strengthen the concepts of justice and equality."[5]

From the corporate side, General Motors spokesman Robert McCabe asserted that "the corporation cannot effectively promote the necessary social and economic change in South Africa if it withdraws from the country."[6] He said that General Motors had improved the lives of blacks it employs: the average wage of GM's black workers was 76 per cent higher than the national average for black workers.

Several business leaders admitted that they could and should do more to bring about change. "Business as usual is not acceptable," said William Broderick of Ford Motor Company, "but moral outrage is not enough."[7]

Some church officials at this conference excoriated Citibank for participating in a consortium that in 1980 made a $250 million loan to the South African government. The president of the National Council of Churches, M. William Howard, said that "foreign bank loans to South Africa act to strengthen apartheid and white minority rule."[8] Wilfrid K. Koplowitz, a Citibank vice president, replied that "banks are not oblivious to moral issues" and that by acting responsibly they could create "a microcosm of justice" in an unjust society. He also pointed out that the loan in which Citibank participated was to be used exclusively for black development projects.[9]

Participants were encouraged by what they felt was an improved climate of exchange and dialogue at this meeting. (Excerpts from remarks at this meeting are found in appendix F.) *New York Times* religion reporter Charles Austin said in the *Christian Century* that "while the differences were marked, the meeting was generally friendly, and church activists are now more aware of the practical problems businesses face than they were several years ago. They understand the problems of expatriating capital and are conscious of the considerable, possibly criminally negligent, loss some companies could suffer if they simply walked away from South African investments."[10]

American churches established missionary activities throughout Africa early in the nineteenth century and have addressed African problems for many decades. Their political involvement is relatively recent, dating from the immediate post–World War II period and increasing in the 1950s as African states were first gaining independence from European control. In 1956 the National Council of Churches called for increased attention to U.S.-African relations. At that time the churches supported both continued missionary activity and an increase of capital investments and development.

More recent church attitudes toward Africa show no decrease in pastoral concern but a substantial increase in attention paid to specific political issues, particularly those involving South Africa. In addition, churches have developed new methods of expressing "social responsibility" in their investment policies. Three major approaches are: (1) dialogue with business leaders, both in forums such as the September 1981 meeting in New York and in personal meetings with corporate executives; (2) shareholder resolutions; and (3) official pronouncements identifying corporations and their practices as objects of particular religious or social concern.

DIALOGUE WITH CORPORATE LEADERS

The meeting of business and church leaders at New York's International House was an expanded version of encounters that take place frequently in corporate headquarters and church offices. Most meetings are not the subject of reports in the *New York Times* or the *Christian Century*; they happen quietly, sometimes with visible results, sometimes not.

A report in *Forbes* magazine in early 1978 described a meeting between executives of Control Data Corporation and representatives of the National Council of Churches and its affiliate, the Interfaith Center on Corporate Responsibility. Reporter Robert J. Flaherty summarized it succinctly: "The whole thing was a fascinating demonstration of how two groups, each equally sincere, can look at the same problem and come up with totally opposed courses of action."[11]

The subject was South Africa, and one exchange was especially illuminating. Control Data chairman William Norris suggested that "if you advocate withdrawal or some kind of partial boycott, you're in fact adding to the increasing unemployment for the black people there and the social turmoil. In a nutshell—the conditions that foment revolution. Are you advocating revolution?"

William Thompson, stated clerk of the United Presbyterian Church and then president of the NCC, answered: "My personal sentiments are with those who are revolting. The people in the streets of Soweto are the George Washingtons of that country. We don't apologize for being on the side of the freedom forces. We've given money and will continue to give assistance to them. . . . I see no hope for evolution in South Africa."[12] (The debate effectively portrays the background of some church policy decisions, and the article is included as appendix G.)

SHAREHOLDER RESOLUTIONS

During the Vietnam War religious leaders learned they could challenge, with some positive results, what they regarded as repugnant corporate policies through shareholder resolutions that corporations had to place before their stockholders for a vote at annual meetings. Using this tactic, religious and academic shareholders condemned Dow Chemical and other firms for their contribution to weapons development and manufacturing. During the post-Vietnam years the use of shareholder resolutions has increased, especially to urge various forms of disinvestment or withdrawal from South Africa.

Although some churches have used this tactic independently, most of them have worked through the Interfaith Center on Corporate Responsibility (ICCR), a coalition of stock-owning religious bodies, whose offices are in New York at the 475 Riverside Drive headquarters of the National Council of Churches. The ICCR membership in 1982 was twenty-two Protestant denominational boards and agencies and twenty-two Roman Catholic religious communities, archdioceses, and coalitions (the latter including some 170 orders and dioceses).[13] The official Catholic hierarchy is not represented. (Drew University theologian Thomas Oden challenges the ICCR claim to be broadly representative of U.S. religious opinion in his 1985 study for the Ethics and Public Policy Center entitled *Conscience and Dividends: The Churches and the Multinationals*.) Church members active in the "corporate responsibility movement," as it is called, believe their convictions should be reflected in the policy and behavior of the corporations in which they or their churches hold stock.[14]

Churches are not insignificant investors. According to ICCR director Timothy Smith, the Catholic orders and Protestant denominations that belong to the ICCR "probably invest over $6 billion." For example, he said, the United Presbyterian Church pension fund is worth approximately $500 million; the United Methodist, over $500 million.[15]

In February 1979 the *Corporate Examiner,* ICCR's monthly newsletter, listed eighty shareholder resolutions or "challenges" under consideration. Nuclear power, television advertising, and infant-formula marketing were three major areas of concern. But the largest number of resolutions dealt with southern Africa and its complex racial problems. Of these, the majority were directed against investment by U.S. firms in the Republic of South Africa.

The issue has continued to be a major one for many American church leaders. In 1981, of seventy-one corporations faced with resolutions sponsored by ICCR-affiliated groups, twenty-seven were being challenged about their business in South Africa. Three firms—Control Data, Fluor, and Sperry—were specifically asked by church-affiliated shareholders to withdraw their investments from the country. Others were requested to stop bank loans or the sale of gold Krugerrand coins minted in South Africa, and Carnation was asked to disclose its marketing and promotional practices for infant formula in South Africa.[16]

By 1982, resolutions filed by Xerox stockholders were able to garner 10 per cent of the proxy vote in a request to end Xerox sales to South African police and military agencies and to declare a freeze on corporate expansion in South Africa. That was the highest percentage of votes received up to that time by a shareholder resolution on corporate involvement in South Africa.[17]

The spring of 1983 saw 119 corporate-responsibility challenges sponsored by church groups through the ICCR. Of these, thirty-eight were aimed at U.S. corporations doing business in South Africa. Six of the thirty-eight were specific requests either for "discontinuing operations" or for "no expansion" in South Africa. The rest asked the corporations to sign the Sullivan Principles, to report to stockholders on South African operations, to discontinue loans or sales to the South African government, or to cease marketing Krugerrand coins.[18]

Shareholder initiatives have met with some limited success. For example, after persistent criticism from the United Church of Christ, one of BankAmerica Corporation's largest institutional stockholders, the company announced a policy prohibiting new loans to the South African government "unless significant concrete steps have been taken to dismantle the apartheid laws." However, this policy (announced in October 1983) does not prohibit loans to the South African private sector. BankAmerica told Audrey C. Smock of the United Church Board for World Ministries: "Withdrawal of credit would not help the non-white population, which is likely to be the group most adversely affected by a decline in economic growth."[19]

PRONOUNCEMENTS BY CHURCH COUNCILS

The third method by which churches express social responsibility through their investment policies is to issue statements on disinvestment. In the rest of this chapter we will look at statements by, first, interdenominational councils, and then individual denominations.

National Council of Churches

The National Council of Churches (NCC) is an ecumenical organization of over thirty Protestant and Orthodox communions in the United States. Founded in 1950, the NCC first voiced concern over South Africa in a 1956 resolution on "American Christian Responsibility Toward Africa." While this statement only briefly mentioned the apartheid problem, the NCC laid the foundation for future statements by insisting that the U.S. government must develop a moral and responsible foreign policy for the entire sub-Saharan region.

In 1963, an NCC pronouncement on "Human Rights" condemned the "particularly vicious form" of racial discrimination found in the Republic of South Africa.[20] The following year, the NCC General Board called on the U.S. government, the United Nations, and "other channels" to pursue a stronger policy of pressure against the South African government, in order "to resolve a crisis which in South Africa is a denial of human dignity and which internationally represents increasingly a danger to world peace."[21] This 1964 NCC resolution first saw investment as a tool of external pressure, and asked member churches "to review their investments in, and their purchases from, South Africa; and, to take effective steps in the economic sphere to support racial justice."

The NCC in 1966 urged the U.S. government to adopt a policy of discouraging trade with and investment in South Africa. It asked that U.S. companies operating in South Africa adopt non-discriminatory policies in employment and personnel assignments. And also, more vigorously than before, it urged churches to examine their investment portfolios and register their protest to any companies that had discriminatory practices.[22]

Not until 1972, however, did the NCC call for withdrawal of foreign investments from South Africa. That year its General Assembly recommended that the member churches "endorse the call of the United Nations, the Organization of African Unity, and the World Council of Churches' Central Committee to foreign economic investors to withdraw from white-ruled South Africa." It further urged that the NCC and member churches use their "stock ownership powers and other strategies to press companies investing in Southern Africa to cease operations and gradually withdraw."[23]

In October 1974, the NCC Governing Board criticized International Business Machines (IBM) for its presence in South Africa. The resolution implied that IBM sales assisted in a build-up of military power by the government and contributed to the continuing repression of the black majority. It called for hearings to be held under the auspices of the NCC and the Interfaith Center on Corporate Responsibility to investigate "possible IBM violations of the spirit or the letter of the United Nations' arms embargo" against South Africa. The NCC Board invited, among others, representatives from the South African Council of Churches, the United Nations, and IBM to testify. The purpose of the proposed hearings was to determine whether the NCC should file a shareholder resolution to call upon IBM "to cease some or all of the operations of its subsidiaries or affiliates in the Republic of South Africa."[24]

In 1975 the Governing Board reprimanded the U.S. government for giving "continued commercial and industrial support to Southern Africa," and claimed that U.S. African policy was one "based on expediency which is not in the best interest of Africa or the United States."[25] In 1976 the Board said that the "heritage of suffering" endured by the black majority in southern Africa required and deserved "recompense more than the possible short-term commercial or material losses of the white minority."[26]

In November 1977 the Board adopted a statement on southern Africa to "take precedence over earlier Council policy in this area."[27] (See appendix H.) In this more comprehensive statement, the NCC made theological and historical points as well as political and economic ones. It condemned racism and said those who defend minority privilege in southern Africa "are imprisoning not only the majority but also themselves."

The Board disputed the claim of U.S. corporations that their investments in South Africa contributed to stability and constructive social change, insisting that "during the decades of expanding U.S. investments, political repression of the African majority has increased." It pressed for an end to economic collaboration between South Africa and the United States in banking, commerce, and industry until black majority rule "is a reality" and urged NCC members to close their accounts in financial institutions that invested in South Africa or made loans to businesses or the government there. The Board also endorsed efforts to discourage multinational corporations from investing in South-West Africa/Namibia "until independence [from South Africa] is attained."

Evangelical Protestant Views

The National Association of Evangelicals (NAE) has as members forty theologically conservative denominations plus individual congregations from more than thirty other denominations. The NAE issues few statements on political and social questions and has taken no position on disinvestment. Its policy is to stay out of international and economic affairs, except in the most general terms of "pursuing moral and ethical policies." According to one spokesman, the NAE generally acts only on request from its member bodies and tries not to speak on their behalf without prior consultation.[28]

Surprisingly, little has been written on South Africa by members of the "evangelical left," or the "radical evangelical movement," which generally espouses evangelical theology but takes more liberal views on political and social questions than other evangelicals.

One evangelical who has taken a stand on South Africa is Dave Fountain, a campus minister at Harvard University, who in 1978 examined the issue in *Sojourners,* a monthly journal of the radical evangelical movement. Fountain reported that Harvard, despite campus demonstrations and student unrest, had decided not to sell its stock as a protest against apartheid. He argued that for Harvard to divest itself of several million dollars' worth of stock would have encouraged other universities, as well as churches and other institutions, to do the same. An action like this, said Fountain, would amount to a "strong argument that it is morally unacceptable for multinationals to maintain a presence in South Africa."[29]

David M. Howard, an American who is general secretary of the World Evangelical Fellowship, has characterized disinvestment as a "very complex issue, not nearly as simplistic as some tend to make it out." He said he discovered on visits to South Africa that both blacks and whites oppose disinvestment because "it ends up hurting those whom it intends to help. It undermines jobs which are usually held by blacks." White South Africans who strongly oppose the government's apartheid policy, he said, "doubt seriously the wisdom or effectiveness of disinvestment as a way to combat" that policy.[30]

State and Local Ecumenical Agencies

State and local councils of churches commonly function only as discussion groups or as clearinghouses for information on public issues; they make no policy statements. The local groups usually focus on topics of local interest. Particular congregations or denominations belonging to the councils sometimes act on national issues on the basis of what they have learned at ecumenical gatherings.

Most state and local councils have therefore taken no positions on South Africa. One exception is Ecumenical Ministries of Oregon, whose board of directors passed a resolution in 1982 recommending that the state of Oregon divest itself of holdings in banks or corporations that do business in South Africa. Ecumenical Ministries of Oregon stated that U.S. investment in South Africa strengthens apartheid "by supporting strategic sectors of the economy and by providing tax revenues" to the government, enabling South African authorities to enforce apartheid laws. Without citing any examples, the resolution claimed that "numerous sources of evidence indicate" that most South African blacks favor disinvestment.[31] A background paper prepared for the group stated that divestment of stock "is a very necessary part of a comprehensive program" to support those seeking change in South Africa. "Without U.S. corporate involvement," the paper asserted, "the range of U.S. policy options toward South Africa would expand."[32]

The World Peace and Global Affairs Commission of the Colorado Council of Churches submitted a resolution on South Africa to the full council in October 1982. "Corporations which continue to invest in and trade with South Africa," it stated, "invariably strengthen" the apartheid system. The commission argued that the Sullivan Principles were inadequate—"at best good intentions and at worst an excuse" for continuing to support apartheid. It urged the U.S. government to join the boycott of South Africa sponsored by the United Nations, and commended the banks and businesses that had already voluntarily "divested from apartheid."[33]

PRONOUNCEMENTS BY DENOMINATIONS

Since about 1970, most major religious denominations in the United States have established standards, procedures, or official committees to guide their corporate investment practices. A primary impetus for this has been the belief that churches should be concerned about the social consequences of their investments and should attempt to influence business to do what is morally right. Several American denominations have adopted policy statements on investment in South Africa.

Baptist Denominations

The **Southern Baptist Convention** is the largest Protestant denomination in the United States with 13.6 million members. It has taken no position on disinvestment.

American Baptist Churches, U.S.A. This 1.6-million-member denomination is an NCC member and closely aligned with mainline Protestant thought. Its General Board issued several resolutions on American investment in South Africa at its December 1981 meeting. The Board argued that "moral persuasion accompanied by economic sanctions has great potential" for bringing about change. It recommended that church officers "utilize divestment of shares" as one way to demonstrate opposition to corporate policy and to apartheid.[34] In another resolution, the Board voted to affirm the Sullivan Principles and to subscribe "to them as guiding principles for the American Baptist Churches in the U.S.A."[35] In a third resolution, the Board directed its general secretary to incorporate the "Sullivan Action Plan"—points made by Leon Sullivan, originator of the Sullivan Principles, in a speech to the Board—into the denomination's investment policy. The plan called on the church to withdraw its funds from banks that refuse to give written assurance that loans to the South African government will be halted until apartheid ends. Likewise, it asked church officials to write all companies in which the church had investments asking that no new expansions be made in South Africa until apartheid ends. If they refuse, the officials should initiate stockholder resolutions calling for an end to new investments; if the companies persist in their policy, churches should divest holdings from those firms.[36]

Progressive National Baptist Convention. This black denomination of 522,000 members has issued no formal statement on disinvestment, but its general secretary, C. J. Malloy, has stated that the convention is unalterably opposed to investment in South Africa. One of its ministers, Representative William H. Gray III of Pennsylvania, introduced legislation in Congress designed to curb U.S. trade with South Africa and reduce U.S investment there.[37] The 1983 version of this legislation (HR 1392) was passed by the House of Representatives as an amendment to the Export Administration Act.

Leon Sullivan, author of the Sullivan Principles, is the pastor of a church in Philadelphia that is affiliated with both the American Baptist and Progressive National Baptist conventions. In 1983 Sullivan said that "the multinational corporations have a major role to play" in South Africa. "It should be the responsibility of these companies to help change that system. Otherwise, they have no moral justification for remaining in South Africa, and should be compelled to leave the country."[38] He urged, however, that until apartheid is ended, "there should be no new expansion in South Africa by American companies, no new bank loans to the South African government, and no sales to the South African police or military."[39]

Lutheran Denominations

In 1977 the **Lutheran World Federation,** meeting in Dar es Salaam, Tanzania, declared apartheid a sin and a heresy; that is, in order to be a member in good standing in a Lutheran church, a believer must reject apartheid. Since that declaration, most member denominations of the Federation have subscribed to the principle, but not without engendering some controversy. Dr. W. A. Visser 't Hooft, one of the founders of the World Council of Churches, said the LWF proclamation was "the boldest step that any international organization" had taken against apartheid.[40] Others were shocked by the LWF move; they thought it placed a political belief on the same level with basic doctrines such as the divinity of Christ. A West German church member asked: "How could the Lutheran World Federation make such an incredible decision and turn a political question into a question of faith? Are all Lutheran representatives of its member churches so filled with hate . . . for South Africa as to be no longer able to distinguish the spirits aright?"[41]

In 1984, the LWF suspended two member denominations, the Evangelical Lutheran Church of Southern Africa (Cape Church) and the German Evangelical Lutheran Church in South-West Africa (Namibia), for their failure to reject apartheid.[42] At the same time, the ninety-nine members of the Federation voted to support "visible and concrete steps," including boycotts and disinvestment, "to end all economic and cultural support of apartheid."[43]

Given the diversity of views in American Lutheran denominations on U.S.–South African relations and disinvestment, the controversial nature of these LWF decisions is apparent. Two major Lutheran denominations, the **Lutheran Church–Missouri Synod** (2.6 million members) and the **Wisconsin Evangelical Lutheran Synod** (407,000 members), have taken no position on disinvestment.[44] This is in keeping with their conservative view of the role of the church in political affairs. Two other denominations, the American Lutheran Church and the Lutheran Church in America (which is an NCC member), have given qualified support to disinvestment.

American Lutheran Church. The 1980 General Convention of this 2.4-million-member church, adopting the Lutheran World Federation's position, declared that apartheid is so serious a sin that "it must be rejected as a matter of the faith itself."[45] Although withdrawing investments is "not a necessary consequence" of that belief, the Convention argued that "at this moment in history in South Africa, divestiture is the most legitimate strategy in opposing apartheid."[46] The delegates called for "withdrawal of investment by United States corporations from South Africa."

In June 1981 the Convention urged U.S. support for United Nations–sponsored economic sanctions against South Africa and proposed that the U.S. government deny foreign tax credits to firms doing business in Namibia. It also encouraged the church's board of trustees to divest itself of stocks in companies doing business in South Africa, as long as "the economic considerations are equal as between two or more securities issues under study." This implies that if the South African–based security were yielding higher dividends than an alternative would yield, it could be retained, despite the moral implications. The Convention also urged that the church refrain from transacting business with banks that make loans to the South African government.[47]

Lutheran Church in America. The 1982 Convention of this 3-million-member denomination (LCA) responded to requests by various local church synods to act on the South African question. In an acknowledgment of complexity that is highly unusual among church bodies, the Convention said that public statements on international issues "must carry a sense of the complexity, interdependence, and constant change that characterize world politics" and must be flexible. "The advocacy of overly simple proposals is in conflict with such a perception of world affairs," it said. "Advocacy of this kind can easily be counterproductive."[48]

After discussing the risks in predicting corporate influence on social situations, the Convention posed a practical question: Would church action calling for disengagement enhance or diminish the church's effectiveness in influencing corporate behavior? "Is it good stewardship" for the church to sell its stock in companies involved in South

Africa as an act of symbolic protest if by doing so it forfeits future influence with those companies?[49]

But without responding to the question, the LCA convention instructed its executive council to (1) "intensify efforts to influence corporations doing business in South Africa to divest themselves of such activity," (2) divest the church of securities, consistent with legal requirements, of corporations "with direct investments in South Africa," and (3) withdraw funds from "banks which make direct loans to the government or para-statal agencies in South Africa."[50]

Richard John Neuhaus, a pastor in the Association of Evangelical Lutheran Churches (107,000 members) and the associate editor of *Lutheran Forum,* visited South Africa in late 1982 and discussed disinvestment in an interview:

> Divestment has a symbolic value: it is another important signal of disapproval. The danger is that it may be another one of those actions which do more to make us feel better than they actually do to remedy an injustice. . . . Among blacks in South Africa, even blacks who are close to the revolutionary option in the African National Congress, there is a private sentiment that divestment is not a major instrument for change.[51]

Although the Lutheran Church–Missouri Synod has taken no official position on disinvestment, in 1982 a denominational magazine (*The Cresset*) published a comprehensive and perceptive analysis in which Arthur Keppel-Jones, a Canadian Anglican cleric and historian, argued that investment by foreign corporations affords the best means of pressuring the government to make substantial reforms. Entrepreneurs and managers in South Africa are demanding that apartheid laws be repealed because they need to open up jobs to skilled blacks and coloreds, he said; otherwise their businesses will be threatened by a manpower shortage. Moreover, blacks gain when the economy flourishes:

> Prosperity improves the lot of blacks and opens the way to further improvement. Conversely, the blacks are the first and worst victims of a depression. If there are no jobs for them in the "white area" they are "endorsed out"—dumped in one of the "homelands" without work or any means of living, but out of sight. The last people to be unemployed are those who have votes.[52]

Keppel-Jones argued that given present conditions, "boycotts and sanctions are probably counterproductive," but that South Africa must never be allowed to forget that the world demands reform. He concluded: "We must not lose sight of the desirable ends; means which will not achieve those ends are not to be adopted merely because they make us feel good."[53]

Methodist Denominations

The 9.6-million-member **United Methodist Church** has been engaged in missionary activity in southern Africa since 1885 and for decades has publicly opposed apartheid. Methodist leadership in southern Africa is strong and visible; for example, Methodist bishop Able T. Muzorewa was the transitional prime minister in Zimbabwe between the regimes of Ian Smith and Robert Mugabe. More South African blacks belong to the Methodist Church than to any other single Protestant denomination.

The 1976 General Conference of the United Methodist Church urged the U.S. government to enact legislation "to forbid any more investment in South Africa and urge similar action by other governments until the apartheid system is ended and majority rule exists."[54]

In 1980, the General Conference adopted a new resolution that urged state and city governments and church financial officers to withdraw funds from banks that make loans to the South African government or government-owned corporations.[55]

The United Methodist Church has supported "liberation movements" in southern Africa and the withdrawal of the investments of multinational corporations.[56] The church's 1984 General Conference in Baltimore affirmed and strengthened the 1976 and 1980 pronouncements on South Africa. Quoting Anglican bishop Desmond Tutu, the resolution said: "Just as the Nazis had final plans for the Jews in Germany, the white South Africans have their final plans for blacks in South Africa."[57]

The Conference also called on United Methodists to "pressure their governments to support United Nations sanctions against South Africa" and to oppose expanded participation of corporations in the South African economy, especially "involvement which enables more efficient police oppression (through computerization) or which promotes the 'homelands' policy."[58]

The resolution called for support of liberation groups such as the South West African People's Organization (SWAPO), and for support of the World Council of Churches' Program to Combat Racism, the South African Council of Churches, and the Council of Churches of Namibia. It recommended that United Methodist parishes, agencies, and individuals withdraw their funds from banks that do business with South Africa and sell their investments in corporations that do the same. It advised against buying Krugerrand coins and called for efforts to boycott "sporting events and cultural personalities which serve to affirm apartheid."[59]

Christian Methodist Episcopal Church. This church has 787,000 members, primarily black. Its 1978 General Conference called for a boycott of gold objects by Americans, since the gold might come from South Africa. It urged the U.S. president to "support the arms embargo and the economic sanctions called for" by the United Nations, and also to "lead Congress in completely severing this nation's relationship with the racist apartheid government" of South Africa. The Conference also declared: "We support the leaders in the liberation movements of South Africa who proclaim that after decades of nonviolent protest, armed struggle is the only alternative left through which they can effect their emancipation."[60]

Although a disinvestment policy would seen to follow from such a strong position, the church has not taken a position on the issue. The church's general secretary, Mance C. Jackson, Jr., wrote that he had "mixed emotions" about disinvestment. He thought that "disinvestment should be supported as a means of withdrawing the economic base from a racist, unjust system." On the other hand, he understood the serious "economic impact of such action on the masses who depend on the jobs provided by American corporations for their livelihoods." This, he said, "poses a real dilemma for me."[61]

Presbyterian Denominations

In 1983 a merger healed the breach between the United Presbyterian Church (north) and the Presbyterian Church in the United States (south), which had split 122 years before over the issue of slavery. The new 3.2-million-member denomination, the Presbyterian Church (U.S.A.), at its 1983 General Assembly condemned apartheid, called on the U.S. government to end all forms of economic support for South Africa, and discouraged economic investment and bank loans until "majority rule is a reality."[62] William Thompson, the church's co-stated clerk, had explained in 1978 that his church (then United Presbyterian) had "come reluctantly to the view that the situation as it now exists in South Africa is not likely to improve by persuasion, and therefore continued economic participation in, and support of, the present regime in South Africa is truly counterproductive in bringing about any improvement in the situation."[63] A brief look at earlier statements by the two separate denominations will lend historical perspective.

United Presbyterian Church. The General Assembly of this 2.5-million-member body issued official guidelines on investment policy in 1971 that advised church officers not to invest in operations that "intentionally or inadvertently support racially repressive or exclusionary regimes."[64]

In 1981 the UPC General Assembly argued forcefully against continued U.S. investment in South Africa. It asserted that multinational corporations "have fortified the economic base upon which the current political structure rests. . . . The net effect of U.S. corporate involvement in South Africa has been to consolidate the power of the minority regime while offering meager compensation to the black majority."[65]

The Assembly also urged the U.S. government to deny export licenses to U.S. firms doing business in South Africa, impose penalties on income earned there, terminate Export-Import Bank credits, exclude South African operations from the insurance program provided by the Overseas Private Investment Corporation, invoke the Tariff Act of 1930 (which prohibits the importation of goods produced by indentured labor), and prohibit the sale of Krugerrands in the United States.[66]

Presbyterian Church in the United States. The General Assembly of this 838,000-member denomination (the "Southern" Presbyterian Church) first addressed the investment issue in 1972. At that time it recommended the use of investment as a tool to achieve justice, urging that "American churchmen devise strategies to influence American investments in southern Africa with the intention of bringing economic justice to the black majorities."[67]

By 1977, however, the Assembly had concluded that investment in South Africa was unethical. It quoted at length a statement of the Christian Institute of Southern Africa (see page 42), whose views on investment were, said the Assembly, shared by other South African black leaders. A passage in the Christian Institute document that "deeply impressed" the Assembly said that "investment in South Africa is investment in apartheid and thus immoral, unjust, and exploitative." Economic growth, the document asserted, cannot produce fundamental change. Blacks are willing to accept short-term unemployment and hardship in exchange for an end to the "suffering caused by the continuation of apartheid."[68]

The 1981 General Assembly reiterated its support for disinvestment, citing the position of the South African Council of Churches and arguing that "foreign investment and loans have been largely used to support the prevailing power and privilege in South Africa."[69] Responding to critics who questioned why South Africa (and not, for instance, the Soviet Union) had been chosen as the target of economic sanctions, the Assembly argued that "while South Africa is not the only repressive regime" that gives businesses and churches cause for concern, "it is the [only] country with substantial U.S. investment which has legalized a system denying the overwhelming majority of people the basic political, social and economic rights on the basis of race."[70]

The Assembly admitted that withdrawing investments cannot alone solve the political problems of South Africa, but said it can be a signal to the government "that business outside of South Africa is not supportive of the government's apartheid policies."[71]

Other Protestant Denominations

The General Assembly of the 1.2-million-member **Christian Church (Disciples of Christ)** declared in October 1977: "We unequivocally support majority rule in South Africa." The Assembly asked Disciples congregations to evaluate their investments in multinational corporations with holdings in South Africa and to act "in ways that will hasten the end of their support of minority rule."[72] The church has co-sponsored stockholder resolutions with other church bodies and ecumenical agencies.

A position paper prepared for the Disciples' Division of Overseas Ministries rejected "the claim of corporations that investments, changes in corporate wages and working conditions act as a force for the fundamental change that is necessary in South Africa."[73] The paper called upon Disciples congregations and other denominations to press corporations to withdraw their investments from South Africa. "As a last resort," it argued, "sale of stock in companies investing in South Africa should be considered."[74]

At its 1983 General Assembly, the church approved a policy for withdrawing church funds from corporations and banks doing "substantial business" in South Africa. The decision did not bind the church to divestment; dialogue with corporations was encouraged as "a first line of action." But local congregations were asked to prepare a process for divestment by 1985 in case discussions with corporate leaders did not lead to the withdrawal of the American firms.[75]

Church of the Brethren. This traditional "peace church," with 171,000 members, issued in 1967 what may be the earliest declaration on disinvestment by an American denomination. It is certainly the oldest still operative as church policy.

The church's General Brotherhood Board, meeting in November 1967, discussed the two "basically different approaches" to reform of South Africa's apartheid policy. The first approach "aims at using and increasing American economic, social, and cultural involvement in South Africa as a means of changing apartheid policy from within." Advocates of this approach argue that the presence of Americans would demonstrate the benefits of non-discriminatory policies and thus help to break down the rigidity of the apartheid system. The second approach aims at "decreasing, terminating, and preventing American economic, social, and cultural involvement in South Africa as a way of pressuring that country from the outside to change its apartheid policy."[76]

The Board seemed to advocate both alternatives. It said that "the presence and practices of the U.S. government and American industries in South Africa could help break down" apartheid.[77] Yet the Board also urged the U.S. government to support "economic sanctions against South Africa" and to "discourage American investment and trade with South Africa."[78] It called on U.S. banks to express American disapproval of apartheid by ceasing to extend credit to the government of South Africa.

When the **Episcopal Church,** the oldest Protestant body in the United States, began examining its investment policy in the late 1960s, it addressed the apartheid issue.[79] The 2.7-million-member denomination in 1971 was the first to file a shareholder resolution on investment in South Africa, one directed toward General Motors.[80]

The 1976 General Convention urged U.S. banks and other businesses "to cease selling goods and services" to the South African government and "not to increase their investments or expand [operations] in South Africa under the present circumstances." It asked corporations to withdraw from South Africa if their presence did not promote human dignity and freedom.[81]

Throughout the 1970s the Episcopal Church in its shareholder actions and in other public forums urged U.S. businesses to observe standards similar to the Sullivan Principles. In 1980, however, the Executive Council of the church's Committee on Social Responsibility in Investments declared that while the Sullivan Principles deserved encouragement, they were not "sufficient goals in and of themselves . . . to induce change in South Africa."[82] At the same time, though, the Executive Council requested both Dresser Industries and U.S. Steel to comply with the Sullivan Principles.[83] John K. Cannon, chairman of the social-responsibility committee, explained at the U.S. Steel annual meeting in 1981 that the Sullivan Principles were better than their native South African counterpart, the Urban Foundation Code, but were at most "a minimum step toward the elimination of apartheid."[84]

Reformed Church in America. This 346,000-member church shares the theological, ethnic, and cultural heritage of the three Dutch Reformed churches in South Africa. All four denominations sprang from the original Calvinist Reformed church in the Netherlands.

The General Synod of the Reformed Church in America declared in June 1980 that the presence of U.S. firms in South Africa "strengthens the apartheid system, postpones liberation, and identifies the United States with the white minority. The benefit to the majority of the people is minimal, while all the people suffer under the system those businesses sustain." The Synod's Executive Committee said that the Reformed Church in America "should encourage those businesses in which it holds investments to end their participation in the economy of South Africa."[85]

The investment policy outlined in the Synod's report is only part of a general policy of support for liberation movements in South Africa and opposition to apartheid. The Reformed Church has been active in pursuing this policy. For example, in 1983 the church filed a shareholder resolution with the Perkin-Elmer Corporation asking it to discontinue operations in South Africa until the government "has committed itself toward ending apartheid."[86]

United Church of Christ. In March 1979 the United Church Boards (of global and domestic social ministries) of the 1.7-million-member United Church of Christ reported on the denomination's corporate-responsibility actions from 1977 to 1979.[87] The study, which may be the most sophisticated and complete analysis of the matter by an American denomination, outlines the means available to church investors for influencing corporate policy. The first is correspondence and personal interviews with corporate executives, a tactic that the United Church Boards had found fruitful on the South Africa issue. If personal discussions are unsuccessful, a second tactic is to submit a stockholder resolution, which, though likely to be defeated, serves to focus attention on the problem. A third tactic, selling stock, was rejected because only shareholders, through their participation in annual meetings, can effectively influence a corporate decision; outsiders are not invited to join in the corporate decision-making process.

The report concluded that the withdrawal of investments from South Africa "cannot be effectuated" and "is not effective." The only effective way to improve conditions in South Africa, it said, is to work through the businesses that now operate there, putting pressure on them to make the country a better place for all its people.

Howard Schomer, an executive of the church's Board for World Ministries, said the UCC had worked diligently to improve conditions in South Africa by encouraging higher wages, union organizing, pension-fund building, desegregation of work and recreation areas, and other reforms. Some church members, he said, had persuaded other shareholders to try to convince corporations to improve employment conditions in South Africa.

The United Church Boards said in the 1979 report that they had tested the strategy of "promoting erosion of U.S. business support" for South Africa, along with encouraging equal employment opportunity for black industrial workers. A mark of success was that over time their shareholder resolutions had gained in proxy support and also in "the support of management." From this they concluded that "at least incremental improvement of the lot of black workers, and even of the corporate witness against apartheid," had occurred.[88]

Roman Catholic Views

The **Roman Catholic Church** at all levels of the hierarchy has repeatedly condemned apartheid. Both Pope Paul VI and Pope John Paul II have publicly stated their opposition to any system of institutionalized racism. *L'Osservatore Romano*, the official Vatican newspaper, on the occasion of Pope John Paul's meeting with Prime Minister P. W. Botha in June 1984, discussed at length South Africa's racial policies and international responses to them. The article pointed out that international sanctions have caused South Africa "to increase its industries in order to become self-sufficient, utilizing and training the black work force that, in the opinion of Progressive Federal Party Deputy Helen Suzman, will hold more important positions during the coming years due to the small number of white workers."[89]

The Vatican has not addressed the investment issue. The hierarchy of the Roman Catholic Church in the United States (51 million members) likewise has no official position on disinvestment. The Committee on Social Development and World Peace of the U.S. Catholic Conference (USCC) urged in a 1976 statement "that the United States use every available means to restrict and discourage U.S. business and investment" in South Africa, Namibia, and Rhodesia (now Zimbabwe), urging "that exceptions, licenses, or mitigations in favor of these nations not be granted."[90] The same statement suggested that American support for international economic sanctions might be an effective way to "give assurance to the government of South Africa, to its black citizens, and to the rest of the world" that the United States still believes in liberty and equality as unalienable rights.[91]

According to Father J. Bryan Hehir of the USCC Office of International Justice and Peace, in 1978 a draft statement was prepared for the National Conference of Catholic Bishops (NCCB) that called for "no further investment" in South Africa; disinvestment was not addressed. The statement was not approved by the bishops, primarily because the Catholic hierarchy in South Africa had not taken a position on the matter. The American bishops decided it would be "wise not to proceed" with the statement without further study. Significantly, no direct communication from the South African bishops *against* taking a position has been sent to the NCCB.[92]

In early 1984 the American bishops issued a statement on "Political Responsibility: Choices for the 1980s," in which they said: "The position of South Africa has long been of grave moral concern to the world because of its internal racial policies. . . . The United States is South Africa's largest trading partner and second largest foreign investor. U.S. foreign policy and its influence on corporate activity in South Africa should be directed in effective ways toward needed change in South Africa and in its relations with neighboring states."[93] Beyond this, the U.S. Catholic bishops have made no recommendations about investment or disinvestment.

Numerous Catholic writers and organizations have taken positions on the issue. Catholic activists, working with others, have had some success in persuading state and local governments to sell their stock in U.S. firms doing business in South Africa and to block the deposit of government funds in banks that lend money to South Africa. In 1982, the Massachusetts Coalition for Divestment from South Africa cited the efforts of religious leaders, and Catholics in particular, as key factors in securing passage of a bill that bars Massachusetts from investing state pension funds in banks that lend money to South Africa. Coalition leader Tom Watkins said that the Massachusetts Catholic Conference "called or contacted every state legislator on this issue before the vote," which overrode Governor Edward J. King's veto of the bill.[94]

The committee on corporate responsibility of the Archdiocese of Milwaukee issued a resolution in 1981 that called upon banks and businesses to "help break down barriers to full participation by non-whites in the South African economy and society." The archdiocese resolved to remove its funds from any banks, specifically Citibank, that lent money to the South African government.[95] Archbishop Rembert Weakland explained that the archdiocese "cannot in conscience receive financial benefit from the kind of evil that is inflicted in South Africa upon its non-white residents." The archdiocese should not, he said, "condone the injustices and discriminations that occur in the areas of health, education, employment, and freedom of movement and speech. Financial loans to such a country will only continue to perpetuate these evils."[96] In 1982 the archdiocese filed a shareholder resolution with IBM asking that company to withdraw its holdings from South Africa; in March 1983 an archdiocesan official reported that since the resolution had received only 3 per cent of the proxy vote, the archdiocese was considering divesting itself of IBM stock.[97]

Father Rollins Lambert, advisor on African affairs to the U.S. Catholic Conference, wrote in *America* in 1977 that "now is the time to cut back on American and other foreign investment in South Africa." He supported this assertion by contending that the ability of corporations to influence social policy and to end apartheid is negligible. He mentioned the great disparity between black unemployment and white unemployment (but did not say how withdrawal of foreign investment would increase employment for black workers).[98] Lambert quoted Bishop James Rausch, then general secretary of the U.S. Catholic Conference, who recommended to the Ford administration that it "use every available means" to restrict and discourage U.S. business and investment in southern Africa; "most especially," added the bishop, restrictions on Export-Import Bank transactions involving South Africa "should not be relaxed in any way."[99] In a 1978 symposium on South African problems in *Commonweal,* a leading Catholic lay weekly, several writers asserted that racism was less the problem in South Africa than capitalism. Peter Walshe, director of African studies at the University of Notre Dame, referred approvingly to the opinion of Beyers Naudé, one of the leaders of the Christian Institute of Southern Africa: "The economic issue relating to capitalism, property, and wealth does in fact constitute the real, deeper problem underlying the issue of race."[100]

In contrast, Lee Tavis, a professor of finance at Notre Dame, argued elsewhere that businesses in South Africa were "a major agent of change," because they had a significant interest in seeing black employees acquire skills and because they were able to grant blacks equal status with whites in the work environment. Tavis thought that businessmen, more than others, understood that economic prosperity and political stability were dependent on full racial integration.[101] Increased Western corporate involvement in South Africa could, he said, lead to steady development based on small but sure increments of social change. Business with its realism and pragmatism is a more effective factor in social change than government with its inertia. "Corporations," said Tavis, "can move people a lot faster."[102]

A leading Catholic activist on South African issues, Father Charles Dahm, O.P., of the Eighth Day Center for Justice in Chicago, who is chairman of the Illinois Committee for Responsible Investment, wrote an article for the Interfaith Center on Corporate Responsibility in 1979.

In it he argued that foreign investment has not improved conditions for blacks in South Africa; that the South African economy is not a sound investment; that blacks in South Africa do not want foreign investment; that U.S. investment in South Africa is significant; and that U.S. investment in South Africa is not apolitical. Dahm reiterated these views at the September 1981 meeting between business and church leaders in New York (see page 47). He argued that since American companies employed fewer than 100,000 South Africans, or about 1 per cent of the country's work force, they could do little for South African workers.[103] (See appendix F for more on Dahm's views.)

The late Reverend Theodore Purcell, S.J., research professor at the Jesuit Center for Social Studies at Georgetown University, opposed disinvestment. This is also the position of the national Jesuit Advisory Committee on Investor Responsibility.[104] Purcell wrote in the *Harvard Business Review* in 1980 that "the churches' focus on South Africa is, in my opinion, out of focus." South Africa's condition is "gradually changing, with some improvements, and American management is having some influence," he said. "It is hard to see clear choices beyond a destructive revolution."[105]

This brief survey by no means exhausts what Catholics have said on these matters. The disinvestment issue serves as a kind of open invitation to repeat popular rhetoric in the face of unpopular facts, and many Catholic leaders have joined the debate. Many Catholics continue to be active in discussions across the country, especially in local ecumenical groups, as states and cities consider legislation that would restrict the investment of public funds in banks and corporations that do business with South Africa.

EVALUATION OF AMERICAN CHURCH VIEWS

As Professor Theodore Purcell said, the churches' focus on South Africa is out of focus. This survey of the policy statements of American religious groups reveals five characteristics: (1) A deep and laudable concern for justice. (2) A tendency to accept myths and half-truths about South Africa. (3) The use of vague and emotion-colored language that often obscures the issues. (4) A disposition to ignore the views of South Africans—including black and white church leaders—who favor increased American and other foreign investment. (5) A tendency to focus narrowly on dramatic schemes or grand gestures instead of gradual paths to change, with the result that the churches fail to translate their legitimate concern into realistic courses of action.

Not all the church statements exhibit all these characteristics; the only component common to all is a Christian concern for justice. Nonetheless, one can draw certain general conclusions from the statements discussed in this chapter.

A prime example of the myths and half-truths that underlie many church pronouncements is their easy characterization of South Africa as a totalitarian or police state with no hope for redemption, short of cataclysmic changes to bring about black majority rule. Most church spokesmen refuse to consider an alternative view, that South Africa is a democratic republic with a severely limited franchise that uses strong legal and police measures against people who engage in activities deemed to threaten domestic peace and order. Another of the prevailing myths is that trade with or investment in South Africa automatically "supports an oppressive regime," even if that economic activity serves to improve the lives of the disadvantaged blacks who are shut out of the political process, and even if it gives them more influence over their future.

A notable example of the use of emotional language is the 1977 statement by the Governing Board of the National Council of Churches (see appendix H). In it, for instance, the whites in Namibia, many from South Africa, are called "an occupation force for the exploitation of Namibia's mineral resources." Actually they are productive managers and workers who, along with black laborers, extract Namibia's valuable mineral resources for domestic use and export. In the same document, the South African government's policy of creating independent black homelands, or "bantustans," is decried as the "'balkanization' of southern Africa." If South Africa were instead trying to do the reverse, to force its sovereignty over nearby independent African states, the government would be rightly condemned for violating the right of self-determination. There are a number of prudential arguments against the homelands policy, but to describe it as "balkanization" is not valid. The word was chosen to evoke memories of the First World War and to suggest that South Africa is following a dangerous path toward destruction.

A similar practice is the use of mutually exclusive categories that identify one group as victims to be saved and another as villains to be reviled. For example, a 1976 NCC statement declared that South African blacks deserve "recompense more than the possible short-term commercial or material losses of the white minority."[106] In a short-sighted way, the NCC omitted from the discussion the related commercial or material losses to black owners of small businesses, black bankers, or black employees of foreign firms. This is what rhetoricians call the fallacy of black or white, which incorrectly splits the consequences of an action into two neat divisions. It elicits the desired emotional response from uncritical or uninformed readers or listeners and thus helps to create irrational or irresponsible policies.

Furthermore, few religious groups in the United States seem to acknowledge the views of South African political and labor leaders who argue strongly against disengagement. They give inordinate attention to the opinions of Bishop Desmond Tutu and the Christian Institute, while ignoring those of many other Christian leaders in South Africa who either reject disinvestment or find it an ineffective means of bringing about social reform. American church leaders seem to be unaware of the views of the many South African blacks who consistently and publicly oppose disinvestment. Ecumenical Ministries of Oregon, for instance, said that "numerous sources of evidence" indicate that "the majority of black South Africans believe foreign investment is harming, not helping, their efforts toward self-determination."[107] These unnamed "sources" would certainly not include such blacks as Gatsha Buthelezi, chief minister of the KwaZulu homeland and a consistent opponent of apartheid, who has said: "Public opinion surveys have shown that the majority of black people support continued investment by Western capital. . . . There is not a single trade union which supports the policy of disinvestment. So I get my cues from ordinary people. The ordinary man-in-the-street in South Africa has never said he is for disinvestment."[108]

Equally significant, few church statements—if any—refer to South Africa's strategic value to the United States and to the Free World. They do not consider what would happen if a regime unfriendly to the West were in power in South Africa during a conflict between the superpowers. The omission of geostrategic issues—the Cape route, the safety of shipping in the South Atlantic and Indian Oceans, and the critical dependence of the West on essential minerals from South Africa—from church statements is a serious and telling one. The preservation of justice and freedom in the West is not a trivial matter. If one result of disinvestment might be the installation of a pro-Soviet government, or a radical-right Afrikaner regime that feels betrayed and humiliated by the West, then all genuinely concerned persons—church leaders, statesmen, business leaders, and ordinary citizens—must consider those possible consequences.

Finally, American church leaders seem to want dramatic, immediate shifts in the power structure of South Africa. They reject—for the most part—the philosophy of Control Data's William Norris: "Everyone's looking for a macrosolution. There isn't one. We've got to get down to the microlevel and grub for each job and save the job you've got. . . . We are talking about overall social change—lighting one candle rather than cursing the darkness."[109]

Catholic theologian Michael Novak added a valuable bit of perspective when he said that while it is indeed a matter of shame that democratic institutions in South Africa represent whites only, and not blacks, the Western observer must remember that "in other African nations, no such democratic institutions exist for anyone. Apartheid corrupts; so does tyranny." The problems, he said, "will not be cured by pious cant."[110]

CHAPTER FIVE

Economic Facts and Political Realities

SOUTH AFRICAN THEOLOGIAN John de Gruchy has urged Americans to be realistic about their role in influencing his country's policies. "Americans don't like to feel impotent," he said, "but it's something you will have to live with. The responsibility for change is ours. Nobody can do it for us."[1] American political analyst Richard Bissell speaks of the "erosion" of U.S. influence on South Africa since the 1960s.[2] With these limitations in mind we can examine what Americans have done and can do to encourage constructive change in a complex, perplexing, dynamic country whose destiny will have impact for good or ill on the larger cause of peace and freedom in the world.

One sign of the widespread appeal of disinvestment is that its supporters include such varied and influential members of Congress as Ronald Dellums, William Gray, Stephen Solarz, and Howard Wolpe. The disinvestment crusade also gained the endorsement of 1984 Democratic presidential candidates Walter Mondale, Jesse Jackson, John Glenn, Gary Hart, and Ernest Hollings.

At other levels of government, too, interest is high. State legislatures, city councils, and pension-fund boards across the nation have acted on proposals to withdraw their holdings in banks or corporations that do business in South Africa. Mayor Raymond L. Flynn of Boston wrote one hundred other mayors in August 1984 recommending that they pass divestment laws, and in September the executive committee of the U.S. Conference of Mayors endorsed the concept as well.[3]

Can the campaign succeed in its immediate goal of limiting U.S. investment in South Africa? If it does succeed, will disinvestment enhance the prospects for a broader political participation by all racial

75

groups in South Africa? In attempting to answer these questions, we must examine the economic and social situation in South Africa, the importance of foreign—in particular, American—investment to the South African economy, and the potential impact of disinvestment.

South Africa, the only industrial state in Africa, has three major economic sectors: mining, manufacturing, and agriculture. The labor force numbers just under ten million persons, more than 60 per cent of them black. Many of the black workers are migrants, working temporarily and often living in urban areas apart from their families in the rural "homelands." Many other blacks have settled permanently in the cities—Cape Town, Johannesburg, Durban, Port Elizabeth—where they work in factories or offices. Still other black workers are not South Africans at all but come from neighboring countries like Botswana or Mozambique, whose economies cannot offer the job opportunities found in the factories of the Cape or the mines of the Witwatersrand.

The blacks, lacking skills and education, have traditionally been limited to low-paying, menial labor, often with little hope for advancement, while whites, coloreds, and Indians have held better paying white-collar jobs. But since the early 1970s South Africa's domestic economy has been changing rapidly as blacks are integrated into the work force as managers, clerks, and foremen—jobs traditionally associated with the "middle class." Steadily increasing demands on economic productivity have led employers to bend or violate apartheid laws. Wage differentials between white and black workers have narrowed; blacks are gaining more economic clout as consumers, savers, investors, and entrepreneurs; and labor unions organized by and made up of black workers have claimed a place at the bargaining table with management and white unions. Together these three economic factors plus increasing educational levels among blacks are transforming South African society.

GAINS IN BLACK WAGES AND CONSUMER POWER

Across the board, substantial wage differences between white and non-white workers still exist, in part a legacy of the long-standing white domination of the political and economic life of the country, and in part perpetuated by white labor unions. Lower levels of job training, language barriers, lack of education, and other factors have also depressed wage levels among non-whites. But overall the wage gap is being reduced rapidly, despite the difficulties of reallocating resources within industries to accommodate higher pay for black workers. Since 1970, the real earnings of non-white workers in industry and mining have been rising more sharply and steadily than those of white workers. The severe recession of 1982-84 slowed this growth, but South Africa's economic record still stands in stark contrast to the wage stagnation in many other developing countries.

Between 1970 and 1979 the wage gap narrowed in all economic sectors, including mining, industry, construction, retail trade, banks, insurance, and government. The rise in non-white income was dramatic in the mining industry, the most visible and important sector of the economy. In 1970 whites earned twenty times the salary of blacks, but by 1979 they earned less than seven times as much. Real wages for blacks tripled between 1970 and 1979. During the same period, many companies provided also for better board and lodging, recreational facilities, and medical services—non-wage "fringe" benefits that further increased the real earnings of blacks—and the government enhanced personal freedom through labor-relations legislation in the late 1970s and early 1980s. Modern, less discriminatory procedures of personnel administration were adopted by many firms, covering activities such as the selection, recruitment, transport, induction, training, promotion, and dismissal of workers.[4]

In some of the professions, blacks, coloreds, and Asians are rapidly closing the gap between whites and themselves. In 1979 blacks in the medical profession were earning 71-79 per cent of whites' salaries, while other non-whites were earning 84-89 per cent. Blacks working in the police administration earned 69-72 per cent of whites' salaries, while other non-whites earned 84-88 per cent.[5]

The shortage of skilled white workers is causing an unofficial but significant breakdown in apartheid laws and practices. Even in the public sector, some civil-service jobs are quietly being filled by non-whites, particularly light-skinned coloreds and black women. In the private sector, the breakdown of the job-reservation system has led to greater parity in salaries and wage-scales.[6] The Bureau of Market Research at the University of South Africa found that average incomes of black households in the Johannesburg area rose 118 per cent between 1970 and 1975, compared to 58 per cent for white households. The five years ending in 1978 saw a 29.5 per cent increase in black per capita income compared to 7.3 per cent for whites.[7]

Per capita income figures for blacks and other non-whites in South Africa now range from two to five times higher than those of blacks in independent black African countries. This explains why one million "guest workers" from neighboring countries choose to work in South Africa. The wages of these temporary laborers from Mozambique, Lesotho, and other African countries often benefit their home countries, because some of these governments insist that 60 per cent of their wages must be sent home.[8] The inflow of this hard currency has been a significant boon to developing countries in southern Africa.

Growing Black Consumer Power

The expanding wage rates (and the diminishing wage gap between blacks and whites) of the 1970s and early 1980s have given the black community, especially in urban areas, increasing economic power. This has forced the government to let blacks in cities and suburbs buy their own homes and to launch a massive electrification program for Soweto, the large black Johannesburg suburb. Etienne Van Loggerenberg of Rand Afrikaans University estimates that in the five years prior to 1982, Soweto household incomes increased by 50 per cent. Soweto's disposable income will soon overtake that of its parent city.[9]

Gatsha Buthelezi, chief minister of the KwaZulu homeland, described the situation: "Jobs bring money to the blacks. . . . Money means power. And working in industry also gives the black man the training and experience he will need to assume his rightful place in our country—just as he did in yours [the United States]. . . . The last thing my people want is to bring industry to a standstill."[10]

The black middle class in South Africa has been growing steadily since the early 1970s, and in 1984 it numbered more than two million. In 1970, said economist Arnt Spandau, the whites' share of total personal incomes in South Africa was 75 per cent compared to 25 per cent for the non-whites. By 1980 the proportions had changed to 60 and 40 per cent. Economic growth had permitted blacks to participate more fully in and to benefit more from their country's economy.[11]

Continuing economic growth means that more and more jobs will be available for black South Africans. Research by economists S. J. Terrblanche and J. L. Sadie of the University of Stellenbosch indicated that by the year 2000 South Africa will need 400,000 persons in executive positions instead of the 170,000 who held such positions in 1983. Given South African demographics—rates of population growth, numbers of persons leaving school and entering the labor force, and similar factors—the researchers stress that that while only 300 blacks, coloreds, and Asians became executives between 1959 and 1979, in the next twenty years nearly 4,000 people from those groups will be needed *each year* to fill new executive positions. Similarly, while in the same period only 8,000 non-whites were added to the highly skilled work force, Terrblanche and Sadie estimate that from 1983 to the end of the century nearly 50,000 non-whites must enter the skilled ranks *annually.*[12] The semi-skilled white-collar positions will also see spectacular growth: while there were 400,000 such jobs in 1983, by 2000 there will be 1.6 million. Many, if not most, of these jobs will be filled by blacks.

RISE OF BLACK LABOR UNIONS

Although blacks have never been legally barred from joining or organizing labor unions, not until the late 1970s were black unions given the same rights to bargain and strike as their white counterparts. Therefore the impact of the black union movement is just beginning to be felt. In 1979, the South African government amended the labor laws to remove job reservations and to open trade-union membership "to all workers irrespective of race."[13] South African law now guarantees all workers the right to work, to organize and join employee organizations, and to bargain collectively; they are also entitled to fair remuneration, equitable conditions of service, access to training and retraining, protection of safety and health in the workplace, security through unemployment insurance and workmen's compensation, and protection against unfair labor practices.

As job prospects for black workers have expanded and wages have risen, black trade unions have grown at an impressive pace. A number of them are grouped in the Federation of South African Trade Unions, which in a single year, 1981, grew from 59,500 to 95,000 members; by 1984 the Federation had 105,000 members. Nearly 100 companies had recognized black unions by 1981, and more than half of all strikes that year were settled on terms favorable to the unions.[14] By 1984, over 600 recognition agreements with black unions were in effect.[15]

As of early 1984, total trade-union membership in South Africa exceeded one million.[16] Blacks accounted for nearly 25 per cent of total union membership in registered labor unions, while coloreds and Asians numbered 31 per cent and whites 44 per cent.[17] The multi-racial but mostly white Trade Union Council of South Africa had 430,000 members in fifty-seven unions. The multi-racial but mostly black Council of Unions of South Africa had an estimated membership of 160,000 in June 1984; at its founding in 1980 the Council had had 29,000 members.[18] The South African Allied Workers Union had a non-white membership of more than 50,000 in twenty unions. Unaffiliated registered trade unions had an estimated membership of 300,000 in a hundred unions. Unregistered black unions had a probable membership of 50,000.[19]

(A "registered" union is one that, in accordance with the Labor Relations Act, has, along with employers in its industry, indicated to the government its willingness to bargain collectively. Unregistered unions may be recognized by employers and engage in collective bargaining, but any agreements reached are enforceable only by the good faith of the parties concerned. They have no recourse to civil protection under the terms of the Labor Relations Act. A union may remain unregistered for a number of reasons, including hesitance to work within the "system," lack of support for registration among the rank-and-file, or too small a membership to promote itself to registered status.[20])

One catalyst for the growth of black trade unions has been the enlightened efforts of many business leaders. Notable among them is Harry F. Oppenheimer, chief of the multi-billion-dollar Anglo American Corporation, who as early as 1974 said: "I do not believe that blacks will ever be brought to accept that the organization of labor which is regarded as right and necessary for white workers, not only in South Africa but throughout the Western world, is not suitable for them."[21] *New York Times* correspondent Joseph Lelyveld has said that black mineworkers' unions, which started organizing in 1982, "would never have even gotten to the gate had it not been for the decision of this archcapitalist [Oppenheimer] to call them into being."[22]

A Strike by Black Mineworkers

Even the gold mines in the Witwatersrand, the last domain of the job-reservation system, have been opened to black unions. In December 1982 the Chamber of Mines, a major employers' organization, announced it would permit collective bargaining with any union that could demonstrate "significant representation" among black workers.[23] The newly formed National Union of Mineworkers recruited 18,000 members in less than six months. Although that figure is only about 4 per cent of the total number of black mineworkers, the achievement was significant. Johann Liebenberg, chief labor officer for the Chamber of Mines, acknowledged that "an irreversible process has commenced."[24] In September 1984, black mineworkers staged their first legal strike; some 40,000 stayed off the job. As a result, the mining companies offered the workers a 16.3 per cent wage increase plus other benefits, ending the walkout. Observers suggested that the success of this strike would lead more workers to join the union.[25]

Black union organizing still faces obstacles. Some white workers and union leaders opposed the 1979 reforms that gave black unions the same rights to organize, bargain, and strike as the older white labor unions. The all-white South African Confederation of Labor, which in 1984 had about 120,000 members, expelled half its constituent bodies for admitting black members.[26] Despite substantial reforms in labor relations and the repeal of the job-reservation laws, some industries still have "closed shops" in which well-entrenched white unions hold the jobs and keep black workers out of their territory. The closed shop is still legal in spite of recommendations by a government commission against it.

Some black union organizers, because their work has a significant political component, are harassed by police and state security agents. Several have been arrested, banned, or sent to the homelands; charges have ranged from simple violations of the Pass Laws to engaging in political subversion or terrorism. Many workers fear they may lose their jobs if they join a union. How much this fear has held down the nonetheless remarkable growth of the black unions is impossible to say.

'Real Progress' For Black Workers

Lucy Mvubelo, general secretary of the National Union of Clothing Workers, South Africa's largest black union, argues that "real progress is being made in labor relations and conditions of *all* (repeat *all*) South African workers. Disinvestment would sabotage such progress and inflict untold hardship and misery on the population as a whole."[27] Mvubelo asserted as early as 1973 that foreign investment—as well as the aid and cooperation of unions around the globe—was needed to undergird the labor movement. She then told the International Labor Organization in Geneva:

> Don't isolate us, don't break off contact, and don't advocate disengagement and withdrawal of foreign investments, because you will still be talking in another ten years' time and the situation in South Africa will not have changed to any degree. . . . Investments from foreign countries have created job opportunities for thousands of African workers who would otherwise have been unemployed. Thanks to the pressure of trade unions in these foreign countries, black workers employed in these foreign companies have recently gained large wage increases, much larger than the wage increase obtained by black workers employed by South African companies.[28]

Irving Brown, director of international affairs for the AFL-CIO, has said that "the existence of a free trade-union movement is the fundamental criterion of whether any political society is democratic."[29] In an essay on South African labor, Professor Roy Godson of the Georgetown University International Labor Program argues that strong trade unions for black workers will "create the potential not only for the emergence of black leaders committed to the democratic process, but also for institutions sufficiently strong to coalesce with others and bring about and maintain democratic change."[30] They do this in several ways, he says. First, unions bring workers together on a non-racial, non-tribal basis in situations where they must cooperate or fail to achieve their goals. Second, union organizing teaches the rudiments of democracy—parliamentary procedure, electoral politics, respect for minority rights. Third, black workers learn that they have an "extraordinary stake in the maintenance of the democratic system" that makes trade unions possible. Fourth, the experience of running large, financially independent organizations gives more blacks than ever before the opportunity to develop leadership skills. Godson points out that a black and multi-racial trade-union movement in South Africa will be similar to the labor movements in Britain, the United States, West Germany, and Israel, where unions became "firm proponents of [democracy], and anchors in a sea of instability."[31]

Ben Roberts, professor of industrial relations at the London School of Economics, has argued that in South Africa's circumstances, trade unions may legitimately use their powers of bargaining and persuasion to seek political franchise for their members. "Throughout their history," Roberts wrote, "in every country where the right to vote was denied their members, unions have used their power and influence to achieve this objective."[32] The peaceful development of industrial relations in South Africa, he noted, is irreversible: "The clock cannot be put back, nor can the hands be stopped without jeopardizing the stability which is essential to the preservation of a [free] society."[33]

The future prospects of this development should not be underestimated. Leon Sullivan spoke of "the growing strength of the black worker [as] one of the greatest hopes for peaceful change in South Africa."[34] Stanford law professor William B. Gould agreed: "One of the best hopes for change in South Africa is through a viable and ultimately strong labor movement."[35] Reinald T. Hofmeyr, director of industrial relations for the Barlow Rand firm, was more specific: "In the absence of other outlets for black political aspirations, it's predictable that trade unions will use the only vehicle in which blacks do have equal rights to press for change."[36] Robert Conway, a visiting scholar at the Harvard Law School Negotiation Project, asserted that trade unions "have the potential to force real change in South African society. The business sector realizes this and is grappling with the new situation. Business realities will have their impact on an outmoded government ideology."[37]

BLACK EDUCATION AND SOCIAL REFORM

"The cause of freedom for all," asserted the South African Council of Churches in late 1984, can be achieved only as people are "trained for the leadership roles they are to occupy one day."[38] The increasing literacy and greater educational achievement that are natural accompaniments of economic gains are themselves forces for constructive change. According to Professor J. P. de Lange of the Rand Afrikaans University, the fact that "more and more black children [are] coming from literate homes" is "the most powerful social factor in South Africa."[39] Literate people more easily become skilled workers and are more likely to become political leaders. More than that, literate blacks in a fairly open society such as South Africa's are predisposed to learn and teach liberal democratic ideas and to allow those ideas to influence political action.

The future of South African education holds great promise, owing in large part to an informal partnership between business and government. Foreign and domestic firms realize that a shortage of skilled workers is more likely to forestall economic growth than a shortage of foreign exchange or domestic capital, and they invest extraordinary amounts of capital in training and educating present and potential workers. American companies are in the vanguard of this effort. U.S. firms that have signed the Sullivan Principles contributed more than $5.5 million in 1981 and 1982 to educate non-employees, and contributed the services of their employees to the educational institutions as well. Control Data, ITT, and Barlow Rand donated a computer-based learning facility to a Soweto adult-education center that serves as many as 4,000 students a night. IBM has contributed almost $3 million to improve science and mathematics programs in Soweto secondary schools.[40] A consortium of American firms gave more than $5 million to build Pace Commercial High School in Soweto.

The South African government, for its part, has increased its expenditure on black education from $83 million in 1974 to $522 million in 1983, an average annual growth rate of 21 per cent.[41] Between 1975 and 1979 the number of classrooms for black students increased from 63,000 to 81,000, while the number of black students rose from 3.7 million to 4.6 million; by 1982 there were 121,000 teachers in 16,000 black schools for 5.3 million black students.[42]

There has been a growing emphasis on adult education "as a second chance strategy for those who did not have access to, or dropped out of, formal schooling," according to K. B. Hartshorne of the University of the Witwatersrand.[43] Dr. Hartshorne reported that in 1983 there were some 340 adult-education centers staffed by nearly 3,000 part-time tutors and attended by more than 38,000 adults. Curriculum at these centers "ranges from literacy courses, basic education programs, through to technical and management skills, to [post-secondary] level programs, for example in language, science, and mathematics."[44]

Most private schools in the country are racially integrated, and the Human Sciences Research Council (a body established to advise the Minister of National Education) recommended in 1981 that public schools also be integrated.[45] The government response to the recommendation, however, was to reaffirm the policy of separate schools for each population group.

ECONOMIC ADVANCES AND RACIAL PROGRESS

Diversifying an economy not only spurs economic growth but also fosters political progress. In a diversified economy, various political and economic interest groups vie for power; social groups that have been outside the mainstream can gain power and influence as choices in the economic sphere increase. Growing personal incomes, spent or saved within these subcommunities, create opportunities for small businesses and lending institutions to develop and expand. A family's ability to own a home promotes responsibility and community stability.

The development of a middle class, or bourgeoisie, has long been recognized by political scientists as a precondition for a working democracy.[46] As Barrington Moore put it: "No bourgeois, no democracy."[47] In South Africa, the burgeoning black middle class augurs well for the expansion of political rights.

Proponents of foreign investment in the South African economy believe that increased economic growth will inevitably alter social structures, leading to greater involvement in the political system by all ethnic groups. Black advances toward greater equality during the 1970s, they say, were due largely to a booming economy. American economist Walter Williams has written:

> Above all, it is South Africa's economic growth that is breaking the back of apartheid. Rapid economic growth makes racial discrimination costly. A growing, robust economy tends to reduce racial hostility and awareness; a declining or stagnating economy does the opposite. After all, can any sane person argue that American blacks could have just as easily achieved the social, political, and economic gains of the 1960s boom during the bust of the 1930s?[48]

Herman Nickel, named U.S. ambassador to South Africa in 1981, made this observation in *Fortune* in 1978:

> In broad historical terms, there appears to be little logic or reason in the idea that economic stagnation provides a better backdrop for the peaceful transformation of South Africa from institutionalized racism into a multi-racial society. The notion would seem all the more bizarre when put forward by Americans, for the whole history of racial progress in the United States points in the opposite direction. Practically every major step forward was linked with economic progress. . . . Economic growth did not strengthen the system of institutionalized racism in the United States; it effectively destroyed it.[49]

Civil-rights pioneer Helen Suzman, who for many years was the most articulate anti-apartheid voice in the South African parliament (and won the United Nations Human Rights Award for her efforts), argues:

> The determining factor [for change] has been—and, I am convinced, will continue to be—economic pressure from within South Africa—the steady upward movement into skilled occupations by blacks, eventually giving blacks the muscle with which to make demands for shifts in power and privilege, backed up by the force of black urbanization, which continues inexorably despite government action to stem it.
>
> . . . If black economic advancement is inadvertently retarded [by divestment], blacks will be the ultimate losers.[50]

Advocates of disinvestment contend that foreign investors lend credibility to an oppressive racial regime and support its policies by their presence. Lawrence Litvak, Robert DeGrasse, and Kathleen McTigue of the South Africa Catalyst Project have argued: "American corporations in South Africa provide a crucial contribution to apartheid. U.S. investment and trade in South Africa create a material bond between U.S. corporations and the status quo regime. This bond, created by profits, provides the minority regime protection from meaningful economic sanctions."[51] British economist Vella Pillay asserted in 1983 that multinational corporations "have certainly forged a close partnership with the South African apartheid state, each supporting the other in their mutual interest of maintaining the black worker as little more than the object of labor, unequal and without rights in his relation to capital and the state, and thereby forced to earn a wage income barely sufficient for him to reproduce his labor and subsist."[52] Trade-union leader Lucy Mvubelo disagrees; in 1979 she said: "The apartheid laws were instituted to create a static situation for the urban blacks but have failed dismally. A healthy and growing economy saw to that."[53]

A related factor noted by Andrew Young, former U.S. ambassador to the United Nations, is that in South Africa, unlike most other countries, the business community is more liberal than the government. Traditionally, white liberals had little hope for career advancement in government service, so they turned to business. Again, a prime example is Harry Oppenheimer, a staunch supporter of the Progressive Federal Party and an outspoken opponent of National Party apartheid policies.[54] Samuel Huntington of Harvard has pointed out that South African businessmen "have been among those most active in attempting to ameliorate apartheid and broaden democracy in that country."[55]

If lasting advances in race relations are more likely to occur amid prosperity than during depression, such advances are also more likely during a time of stability than in one of terrorism or guerrilla warfare, or in the chaos that would follow a violent overthrow of the government. When all racial, ethnic, and religious groups prosper, discontent and resentments among them are minimized, good will increases, and prejudice erodes. The market economy is perhaps the best counterweight to a strong regime, and such an economy will provide the dynamic for political reform.[56]

THE IMPACT OF U.S. FIRMS

Disinvestment advocates Michael Joseph Smith and Stanley Hoffman of Harvard University asserted in a 1983 article: "It is doubtful that foreign investment has improved the position of black workers. The gap between white and black wages is widening, and employment opportunities remain vastly unequal. More and more, the assertion that American investment helps poor blacks smacks of questionable rationalization."[57] Their argument is based on a serious misstatement of fact. As we saw earlier in this chapter, the gap between black and white wages is narrowing, not widening. Further, they assume that U.S. firms invest in South Africa because they are seeking "cheap labor." In the same vein, Litvak, DeGrasse, and McTigue claim "substantial evidence for the view that race relations in South Africa have in large part consisted of the imposition of newer and more refined methods for forcing blacks to labor at a cheap wage."[58] The facts speak otherwise, as Philip Christenson has pointed out:

> The preferred locale of U.S. investment has been in the countries with relatively high wage rates, possibly because the level of wages reflects in broad terms the size of the local consumer market and often a desired level of political stability. . . .
>
> The cheap-labor explanation for U.S. investment in South Africa frequently assumes that labor costs are an important element in corporate investment decisions and an essential element in corporate profitability. The high-wage-area preferences of U.S. investors and South Africa's continuing inability to develop export markets in the labor-intensive product fields (such as apparel and textiles) create doubts about the validity of this explanation.[59]

Indeed, British economist Vella Pillay, who agrees with the "cheap labor" theory of foreign investment in South Africa, has argued that while transnational corporations (TNCs) tend to send their labor-intensive industries to Third World countries where labor is cheap, they do not do this in South Africa: "The TNCs have shown little inhibition or hesitation in transferring technologies of higher vintages—indeed of the 1970s and 1980s—to the more modernizing sectors of the South African economy . . . oil refining, computers, motor vehicles, . . . heavy engineering and automotive processes."[60] These are all capital-intensive, high-wage industries, and they represent the majority of American investments. There are few if any American agribusinesses, which employ mostly unskilled workers, in South Africa.

American firms, more than their European and African counterparts, provide job training for black workers to prepare them for clerical, supervisory, and management positions. In the late 1970s, for instance, Mobiloil South Africa devoted 70 per cent of an annual $1.5 million training budget to black and colored workers; Ford South Africa built a $1 million training facility in Port Elizabeth; and IBM played a major role in operating an "in-service" training facility in Soweto to upgrade the skills of welders, truck drivers, and other workers.[61] U.S. firms also have a commendable record of providing equal opportunity and equal pay for non-white workers. Of all foreign companies, U.S.-owned ones are most often credited with being sensitive to racial issues.

Foreign firms in general have increased their wages for black workers rapidly since 1970, at rates exceeding white wage increases. Many American and other foreign firms provide housing for their non-white employees, who would otherwise have to travel long distances each day to get to work, often from temporary, substandard homes in suburban slums or shantytowns in the homelands.[62]

The Sullivan Principles

As we noted in chapter one, the labor policy of U.S. firms is due in part to the persistent efforts of American civil-rights activists, particularly Leon Sullivan, whose 1977 "Sullivan Principles" were intended "to bring the actions and influences of American companies in South Africa to bear against the racist practices and apartheid laws of that country."[63] Sullivan helped persuade firms from Canada and the European Community, as well as the Urban Foundation in South Africa, to adopt similar codes. His goal is to have one thousand firms adopt the principles.[64] Some of the other codes have gone beyond the Sullivan Principles, including provisions to encourage employers to help black workers buy their own homes near their places of work.

The monitoring agency for the Sullivan signatory companies is the Arthur D. Little Company. According to its sixth report (November 1982), thirty-two firms were "making good progress," thirty-eight were "making progress," and thirty-seven "need to become more active." Evaluations of how the companies were adhering to each of the principles found substantial progress in five of the six. The exception was Principle 5, "increase the number of blacks . . . in managerial and supervisory positions." Most black advancement was from unskilled and semiskilled to skilled jobs; the number of blacks in administrative positions declined, probably owing to the recession of 1981-82.[65]

In 1983 Dr. Sullivan expressed confidence that though progress was limited, his principles were working: "Equal pay for equal work is beginning to be instituted. Companies are beginning to improve the quality of life for blacks and other non-whites outside the workplace in housing, health care, and education. For the first time, some company executives are beginning to lobby for an end to all racial discriminatory laws and the apartheid system."[66]

One problem in implementing the Sullivan Principles is that the monitoring agency is not allowed to visit the workplaces and must depend on information furnished by the firms themselves. Most employers are uneasy about on-site inspection. Darrell Huffman, president of the United States Chamber of Commerce, said in 1980, "It's not normal operating procedure to have strangers wandering around asking questions of employees, because it implies that managers were not telling the truth in their reports."[67] Another problem is that there is nothing to ensure compliance other than public airing of complaints, which may or may not result in improved performance.

Desaix Myers III, executive director of the Investor Responsibility Research Center in Washington, which studies social issues for institutional investors such as universities, has concluded that the response of most employers to the codes of conduct has been "measurable and sometimes impressive. A number of the signers have taken tangible and often dramatic steps towards improving opportunities for black workers." Businessmen in South Africa, he said, have recommended that "all forms of social discrimination written into existing labor legislation and associated regulations be eliminated, and that the principle of freedom of association apply to all workers of all population groups on a common basis."[68] John Chettle, director for North and South America of the South Africa Foundation (an independent businessmen's association), testified to a committee of the U.S. Congress that "most of those [Sullivan-type] principles are now commonplace practice."[69]

Not all observers are so sanguine about the Sullivan Principles. Mark Huber, in an essay for the Heritage Foundation, wrote that the code had "turned into a bureaucratic quagmire and created a controversial backlash with major foreign and domestic policy implications."[70] S. G. Marzullo, a Mobil Oil Company executive and chairman of the Industry Support Unit (which helps oversee compliance with the Principles), noted that the rating system employed by Arthur D. Little suffers from several shortcomings. "The present questionnaire only partially reflects what companies are doing," he said. "In effect, it's a shotgun approach to 'What do you do to help non-whites in South Africa?,' with each company trying to make as many points as it can to get a good grade. We need a questionnaire that deals with how you address basic root problems."[71] Marzullo also pointed out that the Sullivan Principles created excessive expectations. He insisted that they must be viewed as a long-term program. A company "may fall back during a reporting period and then go back up again," he said. "It isn't fair to penalize them over the short term for some temporary setbacks."[72]

Efforts to Legislate Compliance

Attempts made in the U.S. Congress to legislate mandatory compliance with the Sullivan Principles have met opposition from both the executive branch and business leaders. In a State Department memorandum, its legal advisor's office listed severe problems posed by such legislation, noting that the department "has neither the resources, the expertise, nor the organizational infrastructure necessary to perform the large-scale economic regulatory function assigned to it by the proposed legislation."[73] The memorandum added:

> The Sullivan Principles are extremely comprehensive; their codification . . . would necessitate detailed examination by the State Department of virtually all aspects of a firm's employment policy. At the same time, the Principles are in many respects too vague to permit ·a definitive judgment of full compliance. The Sullivan Principles were formulated and drafted as a set of voluntary guidelines for firms doing business in South Africa. They were never intended to provide a set of standards sufficiently precise to be applied as law. Although very useful as guidelines for voluntary action—and strongly endorsed as such by the United States Government—the Sullivan Principles would be difficult for a judicial . . . tribunal to interpret and apply as legal standards.[74]

Most important, the character of the proposed legislation would be at variance with "accepted notions of the limits to 'extraterritorial' applications of a state's law." In other words, mandating the Sullivan Principles is beyond the jurisdiction of U.S. law.[75]

Business spokesmen, too, have objected to this legislation, which is embodied in amendments to the Export Administration Act proposed by Congressmen Stephen Solarz and William Gray. Ford Motor Company executive William Broderick called the amendments "a bureaucratic monstrosity."[76] General Motors has insisted that the principles work best "because of their voluntary nature"; a legal mandate would erode this advantage.[77] S. G. Marzullo of Mobil warned: "In the long run [the proponents of the amendment are] hurting the people they want to help."[78]

The Sullivan Principles, as voluntary guidelines, are useful and worth extending. They should not be seen as the sole reason for the progress in equal opportunity for non-white employees, however. Many other factors—such as the clamor for equal pay by South Africans, the economic benefits of improved social conditions for American business, and the expanding market among South African blacks—contributed to the pressure for reform. Howard Schomer, a financial consultant and United Church of Christ minister, argues that "foreign corporations can make a substantial and *very direct* contribution by helping to provide an equal opportunity for all citizens to secure everything necessary for their economic well-being."[79]

South Africans Speak Against Disinvestment

The combination of South African economic conditions that portend a broadening of democracy and U.S. corporate practices that generally benefit black workers and their families has led many leaders from all of South Africa's racial groups to oppose disinvestment and other economic sanctions. Political, religious, and labor leaders have announced their belief that sanctions would be of dubious value, and might in fact be detrimental.

Opposition From Labor and Business Leaders

Lucy Mvubelo is the most outspoken black labor leader with this view. She points out that retarded economic growth "can also affect the whites, and the old story of jobs for whites will once again become a major issue. Repressive laws will again be demanded."[80] She contends that "those in our country who urge a boycott of South African goods and the disinvestment of Western capital are simply a small fringe of desperate revolutionaries. They realize that the basic condition from which revolution can arise does not exist; thus the world must create it."[81] (An elaboration of her views may be found in the foreword to this volume.)

Those who would suffer most from disinvestment are the black workers, especially those who are just beginning to enter the skilled labor market. Fred Sauls, a union organizer for black auto workers, complained: "It's all very well for people to urge disinvestment who sit in safe comfort in some nice office 8,000 miles away. But if the American auto plants here closed down, I'd have thousands of men . . . wondering where the next meal would come from."[82]

Zulu chief Gatsha Buthelezi is the leader of Inkatha, a multi-ethnic political-cultural organization with more than 750,000 members; U.S. theologian Richard Neuhaus has called him "the most credible black leader in South Africa."[83] In a 1983 interview Buthelezi said that although the free enterprise system "has not made the black people of South Africa free," because in some ways they are excluded from it, at the same time "when I see my people lining up for jobs in Johannesburg, Durban, and other metropolitan areas of South Africa, then I must say that my people vote with their feet for the capitalist system."[84] Buthelezi, who opposed the 1983 constitution, added:

> I cannot theorize about disinvestment. Others can afford to theorize in their board rooms or to write about it. I believe apartheid is a scourge that should be wiped off the face of the earth. But at the same time I do not believe that there will be any disinvestment. Pressure has brought about changes insofar as some corporations have moved in the direction of economic justice for black people.[85]

(A longer statement by Buthelezi is included as appendix I.)

Llewellyn Mehlomakulu, a black banker from Soweto, has pointed out that "the view of the South African black silent majority is never given the same kind of publicity as the pro-disinvestment viewpoint. The majority of blacks in South Africa is for continuing U.S. business involvement providing that it contributes to evolutionary change. . . . If the United States pulled out, you would lose your leverage for change."[86] Mehlomakulu noted that in meetings he had had with Roy Wilkins, leader of the U.S. NAACP, Wilkins affirmed support for investment in South Africa and said "involvement was desirable."[87]

S. I. P. Kgama, a founder of the Urban Councillors Association of South Africa, said that disinvestment "will cost us jobs. At the present time, there are ten blacks seeking every job which comes available. Those who advocate disinvestment want to make things worse so that the people will be radicalized. But history shows that power gained by violence is never freedom. It becomes a kind of oppression."[88]

J. N. Reddy, an Indian businessman, said that despite the urgings of those who want revolutionary changes that "will inevitably destroy the very infrastructure" required for the economic development of the black, colored, and Asian communities, "the overwhelming majority of South Africans of all racial groups are committed to a process of change through peaceful means."[89] Foreign businesses play a role in this process, Reddy argued, by helping to support housing and education projects and by extending support to businesses owned and managed by non-whites to enable them to overcome "historical impediments" and become part of the free enterprise system.[90]

Another Indian, attorney Pat Poovalingham, who chairs the Solidarity Party, said in 1978 that disinvestment will cause "fewer jobs, more poverty, greater hunger. More frustration, greater interracial hostility." Disengagement, he said, "will hurt the whites. Of course it will. Inevitably. Inescapably. But last. First to be affected will be the blacks. Then the browns [coloreds and Indians]. And finally the whites. Until the violent revolution, for which the Communists have carefully prepared the scenario, becomes inevitable. Is this what the liberals in the United States really want?" If there is economic disengagement, Poovalingham asserted, "the movement toward mutual discussion that is taking place in South Africa will be halted."[91]

Opposition From Workers

South Africa's workers—poor and middle class—reject disinvestment. Suzanne Garment observed in the *Wall Street Journal* during a trip to southern Africa: "When you ask about [disinvestment] here, almost all black and white anti-apartheid activists look at you like you're crazy. They cannot imagine why you would want to threaten the economic growth that has been the chief engine of racial progress and of the current South African political ferment. It's not easy to come up with an answer."[92]

A survey of black South African workers conducted in 1984 by Lawrence Schlemmer, president of the anti-apartheid Institute of Race Relations, found that 75 per cent of the workers opposed disinvestment. Fifty-four per cent said it would reduce the number of jobs, and 41 per cent said that it more generally would harm blacks.[93] Professor Schlemmer said the remaining 25 per cent "were definitely not in favor of unqualified disinvestment."[94] He concluded: "Whatever its validity as a means of providing opposition to vested white interests and structures, [disinvestment] cannot claim to be a campaign for the black rank-and-file people of South Africa."[95]

Correspondent Alan Cowell, writing in the *New York Times*, noted that the survey's findings "seem certain to fuel the dispute over divestment since they seem to undermine those radical groups, most prominently in exile, such as the African National Congress, that argue in favor of the withdrawal of American investment."[95] Cowell wrote that the workers' opinions appeared to support moderate black movements and the Reagan administration's policy of "constructive engagement" as the best means to bring about reform. Schlemmer said the survey showed that for black South African workers, "the presence of U.S. capital . . . is highly valued."[97]

Schlemmer did find a significant level of discontent among the workers surveyed—two-thirds described themselves as angry or impatient. He had expected more of this discontent to translate into support for disinvestment.[98] Instead, he found that black workers realize they have a stake in the South African economy and are reluctant to jeopardize it. "Disinvestment by U.S. companies and trade sanctions are a threat to their material and work interests, and therefore they oppose them with a firm consistency."[99]

DISINVESTMENT: THE PROBABLE IMPACT

If withdrawing U.S. corporations from South Africa seriously disrupted the South African economy, as disinvestment advocates contend it would do, this would not help the process of constructive change. Herman Nickel noted that the "true nature and impact of any economic disengagement or withdrawal would bear little if any similarity to the avowed objective of its ardent advocates. And this essentially is why the vast majority of companies—after sober weighing of all risks and uncertainties—have chosen to stand their ground."[100] In 1984, Progressive Federal Party member Robert Conway argued in *Worldview* that the United States should declare itself "totally opposed to the divestiture and disinvestment movements, which are completely counterproductive." He asked: "What can be more immoral than for those who are thousands of miles away from suffering to condone the policies that bring it about? South Africans do not want further hardships for blacks, and such action would have a detrimental effect on the forces for progressive change." The United States "should encourage increased American investment in the area," he said, working towards "greater business contact, not less."[101]

Proponents of disinvestment insist that economic sanctions can force South Africa to change its evil racial policies and its hostile policies toward neighboring states. Litvak, DeGrasse, and McTigue put the case this way: "U.S. corporate involvement in South Africa strengthens the status quo and encourages complacency among whites regarding fundamental political change. The withdrawal of American firms would weaken this status quo and create hope among black South Africans that they can effectively challenge the regime."[102]

Those taking this position are generally aware that withdrawal of Western capital might cause economic dislocations of a kind that could create conditions conducive to revolutionary violence. American political analyst Richard Bissell has written that their belief that economic sanctions would "precipitate a political crisis in South Africa is accompanied by a faith that it would bring forth a black-ruled state with significantly greater virtues than the present system in South Africa (or any system likely to result from the present direction of reform in South Africa)."[103] They think such turmoil could, at the very least, drive the present National Party regime out of office.

The general economic consequences of disinvestment have been described by German economist Arnt Spandau, formerly a professor at the Witswatersrand University. From projections of data current in 1976 he concluded that a 20 per cent "investment boycott" against South Africa—that is, approximately the proportion of U.S. investment among foreign investors—would cause unemployment to rise "by about 37,000 persons, 30 per cent of whom would have been white and 70 per cent non-white. Hence, in terms of the number of work places lost, non-whites would have been hit harder than whites."[104]

Disinvestment and other sanctions would certainly have a negative effect on several black African countries. John Chettle suggested that "some neighboring states would probably suffer more from sanctions against South Africa than South Africa itself."[105] All the states of southern Africa are economically interdependent, and South Africa is the hub of the network. David Lamb, a Nairobi-based correspondent for the *Los Angeles Times,* wrote in his book *The Africans* that "black Africa depends on South Africa. Without it, national economies in the southern third of the continent would fall like dominoes."[106] Southern African countries import much of their food from South Africa, and landlocked countries such as Zimbabwe and Malawi must ship their own products through South African ports. Thirty per cent of the

Botswana work force in 1981 was employed in South Africa; during the same year, 150,000 of 180,000 gainfully employed citizens of Lesotho worked in South Africa.[107]

Yet past experience with economic sanctions casts doubt on their proponents' position; it indicates they do not have the desired effect. The authors of *Economic Sanctions in U.S. Foreign Policy* say "that economic sanctions have not necessarily altered the positions of the targets and in the long run have been ineffective in the fulfillment of their objectives."[108] One reason for this—isolation—may be especially appropriate to South Africa. Researcher Margaret Doxey found that in every case she examined, economic sanctions failed because international ostracism limited communication with the target country and made understanding more difficult to achieve.[109] This is a likely result of the increased isolation of South Africa by the international community in sports, diplomacy, and business. Richard Bissell states flatly that sanctions alone, without military confrontation, "cannot persuade the increasingly self-reliant South African society to change race legislation and the constitutional dispensation."[110]

Moreover, it is unlikely that U.S. disinvestment would have the profound effect its advocates have claimed since U.S. direct investment in South Africa represents about 20 per cent of total foreign investment, and only 4 per cent of the total capital invested in the South African economy. South Africa's economy is closely tied to that of Western Europe. The European Community, or Common Market, nations account for 57 per cent of foreign investment in the nation; any economic boycott would require their support, and such chances are remote. Even the strongly anti-apartheid British Labour Party, when it was in power from 1974 to 1979, refused to pull British firms out of South Africa. The Labour government recognized that at least 70,000 Britons would lose their jobs as a result of economic disengagement. The prospect is similar for other European countries, and for individual foreign investors as well.

Politically and economically devastating consequences could hardly result from the withdrawal of American investment alone. The $2 billion in U.S. investments—less than half the amount held by British firms—is not enough to make a significant difference. There are just over 300 U.S. companies with South African subsidiaries in contrast to nearly 6,000 firms from other countries that do business there.[111] Non-American firms have more employees, more contact with South African business, labor, and political leaders, and accordingly more potential influence on society and politics there.

There is, moreover, the near certainty that American firms, pressured to disinvest, would sell their assets to eager British, Swiss, West German, or South African entrepreneurs. As marketing professor Robert Weigand said in the *New York Times,* "one can almost hear managing directors in other countries holding their collective breath in anticipation of windfall profits brought by an American pullout."[112] There is reason to fear that employment policy toward blacks would be less enlightened under non-U.S. ownership, and that the whole American initiative toward fair labor practices would be significantly eroded. Consider what union leader Fred Sauls said about the treatment of nonwhite employees: "Most of the American firms are pretty good, certainly a hell of a lot better than the British firms."[113]

Nonetheless, the debate continues, and many people—in the churches, for instance—insist that economic sanctions and disinvestment are the best way to bring about constructive change in South Africa.

CHAPTER SIX

The Churches and South Africa: Toward Greater Effectiveness

AMBASSADOR JEANE KIRKPATRICK has noted an ironic twist in the attitude of the U.N. General Assembly toward South Africa and multinational corporations. The United Nations, she says, is caught up in a "crude kind of anti-capitalist ideology," one that sees multinational corporations as "very bad institutions" that harm the countries in which they operate. But "there is a single exception to this: it is also assumed, when the question of investment in South Africa is considered, that multinational corporations *help* South Africa." Only here do U.N. delegates see corporations as economically beneficial to the country in which they operate.[1]

Withdrawing or reducing external investment in South Africa is likely to do one of three things: (1) have little or no effect on the politics and economy of the country; (2) prod the Pretoria government to relinquish power to a black-controlled regime; (3) cause economic dislocation, unemployment, and hunger, and thus precipitate a violent revolt against the government, which may or may not lead to its overthrow. Labor leader Lucy Mvubelo thinks the first two eventualities are unlikely and told an interviewer that if there were a full-scale withdrawal of Western capital, "clearly the greatest hardship would fall on my people, the black people. They will be the first to lose their jobs. They will be left to die of starvation. They will be the first to be killed in a revolution."[2]

Canadian historian Kenneth Hilborn has commented on the connection between hunger and violent revolution: "Lenin once opposed a famine relief effort for Tsarist Russia, on the ground that hunger and misery among the masses would serve the cause of revolution. Similarly, by contributing to unemployment and hardship among South Africa's non-white population groups, especially blacks, economic sanctions might well drive many to desperation and therefore to violence. In this way people who would prefer to live and work in peace could be turned into cannon-fodder for the revolutionary war that so-called 'liberation' forces hope to launch."[3]

Evaluating the Churches' Stands

In chapter one we posed several questions about the ethics, empirical validity, and intellectual integrity of church positions on investment in South Africa. The three chapters that followed examined and assessed the statements and actions of the World Council of Churches, South African churches, and American churches. In the light of these data and the empirical analysis in chapter five, we will consider four questions about church pronouncements: (1) Do they properly relate ends, means, and consequences? (2) Are they true to their religious traditions? (3) Are they based on solid empirical evidence? (4) Do they take a single-issue or multiple-consideration approach?

1. Relating Ends, Means, and Consequences

Some Christians support disinvestment and divestment tactics in the belief that economic pressure alone may force the Pretoria government to extend full political rights to blacks. But disinvestment is not a likely means to that end. As Richard Bissell pointed out (see page 97), there is little possibility of forcing concessions from the government without sustained military pressure along with economic sanctions.

Many opponents of American investment hope that economic pressure on South Africa will lead to revolution. But violent overthrow of the government is unlikely to produce the desired end of greater justice and freedom for all non-white South Africans. "When in world history," asks Samuel P. Huntington, "has violent revolution produced a stable democratic regime in an independent state?" Except for Costa Rica in 1948, he asserts, never. "All revolutionary opponents of authoritarian regimes claim to be democrats; once they achieve power through violence, almost all turn out to be authoritarian themselves, often imposing an even more repressive regime than the one they overthrew."[4] Yale political scientist Robert A. Dahl states that stable democracies "are more likely to result from rather slow evolutionary processes than from revolutionary overthrow" of existing regimes.[5]

Evolution toward greater justice in South Africa is certainly possible and by most accounts inevitable. As Samuel Huntington has said, the prospects for democratic development are greater there than elsewhere in Africa where "majority rule" has already been achieved.[6] The mere presence of members of the majority racial group among those who have attained power has hardly been a guarantee of human rights or the extension of democracy in Africa or elsewhere in the Third World. As a slogan, "majority rule" is quite appealing; the sad fact is that such sloganeering has led to bloodshed in other African countries far worse than any of the tragic events that have occurred in South Africa since it became independent.

Another shortcoming of the church documents is their failure to acknowledge the possible adverse consequences of a chaotic or revolutionary South Africa for the security of the United States, Europe, Japan, Canada—indeed, the whole Free World. If the present government remained in control, the possibility that it might take retaliatory action against boycotts or other sanctions should be taken into account. As C. Fred Bergsten, an assistant treasury secretary during the Carter administration, testified, "the United States is more vulnerable to South African economic sanctions than South Africa is to U.S. action. The hard fact is that South Africa has more cards to play than we do in this area."[7]

Of greater security concern is the possibility of a revolutionary regime in Pretoria with interests inimical to those of the United States and its allies. Both because of its resources and because of its location, South Africa is vital to U.S. security. Retired admiral Robert J. Hanks has written that "Free World policies toward that beleaguered state will determine, in large measure, the eventual outcome of the Soviet-initiated struggle for control of access to the raw material riches of southern Africa."[8] The West and a number of African states (Zaire, Zambia, and Zimbabwe) have a great stake in seeing that South Africa remains free from Soviet control. "Highly important to Free World peacetime economies," Hanks noted, "this international factor assumes critical significance in time of war, given the indispensability of these cargoes [South Africa's minerals and Middle Eastern energy supplies] to weapons production, not to mention combat operations."[9] For the Cape of Good Hope to be in friendly hands is of crucial importance to naval operations and the safety of sea-going freight between Europe, the Far East, and America.

2. Fidelity to Religious Traditions

Direct or indirect support for violent revolution is contrary to the standards of the Christian just-war tradition. The World Council of Churches declared in 1948 that "war as a method of settling disputes" is incompatible with the Gospel of Jesus Christ, but now it actively supports—with money, personnel, and public pronouncements—terrorist groups seeking to overthrow the South African government through subversion, terrorism, or guerrilla warfare. Churches in the United States and Europe that have given money earmarked for the Program to Combat Racism thereby support revolutionary movements in southern Africa that have caused the deaths of hundreds of innocent civilians, including some missionaries.[10]

A call for actions that cause economic dislocation and distress is a call for creating the conditions that may lead to violent revolution, with its accompanying terror, repression, death, and possible dictatorship. Church activists who support disinvestment or divestment movements within their denomination, or lobby for legislative action in state capitals or the U.S. Congress, should ask themselves: "Is my position consistent with the ethics of war, peace, and revolution taught in my religious tradition?" If the answer is no, they must consider alternative paths to constructive change in South Africa.

Pope John Paul II disputed the claims of some liberation theologians and reaffirmed the Christian moral teaching in a message to the bishops of southern Africa gathered in Harare, Zimbabwe, in August 1984. "The solidarity of the church with the poor, with the victims of unjust laws or unjust social and economic structures, cannot be dictated by an analysis based on class distinctions and class struggle," he said. "The church's task is . . . reconciliation, without opposing groups, without being 'against' anyone."[11] The Vatican Congregation for the Doctrine of the Faith, in a major statement on liberation theology, insisted that the battle for justice "be fought in ways consistent with human dignity. That is why the systematic and deliberate recourse to violence, no matter from which side it comes, must be condemned." To trust violence in the hope of restoring justice, the Vatican document said, is illusory. "Violence begets violence and degrades man. It mocks the dignity of man in the person of the victims, and it debases that same dignity among those who practice it."[12]

Earlier, Pope John Paul had told members of the U.N. Special Committee Against Apartheid that efforts to eliminate apartheid were "delicate" and demanded "firmness in the choice of means." The church, he said, would support "every effort aimed at removing the temptation to violence" in that struggle.[13] This rejection of violence and espousal of constructive, peaceful change is conspicuously absent from the statements and activities of the World Council of Churches and most U.S. denominational statements. ˅

3. Scope of Evidence

With a few exceptions—most notably the United Church of Christ and the Lutheran Church in America—the churches have failed to consider (perhaps even deliberately ignored) alternative points of view in their pronouncements. As we saw in chapter two, the World Council of Churches said flatly that those who support evolutionary change are supporters of apartheid and racists. Most American church documents cite only the Christian Institute and Bishop Desmond Tutu as South African authorities. The evidence in chapter three shows that these sources are not an accurate reflection of South African religious opinion.

Furthermore, no American church document made reference to the views of South African trade-union leaders, members of the opposition parties such as Helen Suzman or Robert Conway, or black leaders like Gatsha Buthelezi, who consistently have opposed *both* apartheid *and* disinvestment and related tactics of isolation. And the available public opinion data are not reflected in the churches' statements.

The absence of economic data, the abandonment of traditional approaches to revolution and violence, the easy dismissal of probable adverse consequences (both for black employment and wages, and for the security of the Free World), the failure to consider a representative range of South African views, and the unwillingness to admit that revolution almost always leads to oppression—all these are serious flaws in the churches' pronouncements.

4. Breadth of Approach

One of the principal reasons why the church statements fail the test of integrity is that they doggedly take a single-issue approach to a highly complex problem. The pronouncements typically assert that there is *one* problem in South Africa—apartheid—and that economic sanctions and disinvestment are the best or only means to solve that problem. The problem of South Africa has multiple causes—historical, political, racial, linguistic, religious, geographic, and military. To put forth majority rule as the single end and disinvestment as the sole means to that end and to ignore other likely consequences of disinvestment is morally irresponsible and politically ineffectual.

RECOMMENDATIONS TO THE CHURCHES

Church leaders and organizations have a right and obligation to speak out on public issues, but they have an equal obligation to speak responsibly. How can they improve the moral quality, intellectual substance, and political relevance of their pronouncements on U.S. government and corporate policy toward South Africa?

First, church leaders need to be better informed about the political and economic facts. Too often they accept the false notion that South Africa is a repressive, totalitarian country similar to Nazi Germany. In fact, the country is diverse, pluralistic, dynamic, and rapidly changing. There are many forces within the government, the churches, the economy, and South African society as a whole that lend themselves to further liberalization. Denominational leaders, clergy, and parishioners need a broader picture of South African life and opinion. Exchanges between American and South African students and clergy would help provide useful information.

Churches should continue their efforts to persuade corporations and banks to adhere to equal-opportunity codes, such as the Sullivan Principles. They should rely on moral persuasion through dialogue with business leaders rather than threats of divestment or boycotts. Churches should encourage prudent U.S. investment in black development projects and loans to black-owned businesses. Churches can help corporations initiate and operate programs to bring South African students and workers to the United States to further their education and training. They can encourage American firms to patronize black-owned South African companies that offer needed products or services at competitive prices. Also, through their traditional ties with the labor movement, churches can offer support and encouragement to the newly emerging black unions.

The U.S. corporate presence in South Africa, though certainly not above reproach, is a force for good. Most U.S. firms advance the cause of human dignity. They increase the material well-being of workers and their families, they adhere to non-segregation standards that break down the walls of apartheid, and they invest in community projects that promote human development. American firms teach their black and colored employees the managerial skills useful for community leaders of all sorts—in the church, in the broader business community, and in politics. Many firms have come to realize that in making a profit on their capital investment they can also invest in greater justice and freedom.

American churches should therefore oppose actions by federal, state, or local governments to limit U.S. business in South Africa. On the contrary, they should encourage the expansion of U.S. business there because American firms contribute to productivity and prosperity and thus help create a climate for constructive change.

The churches should also oppose terrorist movements bent on destroying South African government or society. The country has an independent judiciary, a remarkably free press, active human-rights groups, opposition political parties, and an electoral process that permits change. To support revolution despite the presence of effective channels for peaceful change is not only counterproductive but also immoral. Assistance to terrorist groups will only force the South African government to become repressive to ensure its own survival. This is a prospect that no one—black or white, American or South African—should desire.

Churches should pay more attention to strategic considerations. The stability and continued productivity of southern Africa is vital to the security of the West, which depends on South Africa and its neighbors for minerals critical to military deterrence and necessary to maintain a strong international economy. Moreover, South Africa overlooks the shipping lanes that Europe depends on for its petroleum. Control of these lanes between the Indian and Atlantic oceans would be a prime target in a war between the superpowers. The churches should be aware

of the strategic consequences when they support any movements—
revolutionary or otherwise—that might topple the presently stable and
friendly regime in South Africa.

Baldwin Sjollema, former director of the World Council of
Churches' Program to Combat Racism, has suggested that Christians
have a duty to continue to study the South African situation, to publish
reports on politics, economics, and civil rights, and to act on the
knowledge so gained. This book is meant to be a contribution to that
effort. The United States and South Africa share similar histories of
settlement and development; we share the experience of wrestling with
the evils of slavery and racial discrimination; and we share a commitment to the Western ideals of limited government and the rule of law.
For Americans to rupture these bonds through misunderstanding or
through support for revolutionary change would be a tragedy for both
countries.

South Africa is one of the world's most promising countries—
dynamic, rich in material wealth, rich in culture and people, rich in
political and economic institutions. Its problems are not so complex as
to defy solution. What outsiders should ask for is not perfection but a
serious effort to provide basic civil rights and economic opportunities
for all citizens.

Christian ethics teaches us the value of each individual. It also
teaches the value of cooperation—none of us stands alone. Isolating
South Africa and its people from the economy of the West is no
solution to the complex racial and political situation in that country. It
can only exacerbate tensions and lead to greater poverty, injustice, and
violence.

Per Capita Income in South African Racial Groups and Selected Countries

The figures in this chart are not exactly comparable, since they come from several sources and are for different years within the period 1978-82. They do provide a rough basis for comparing the incomes of various groups within South Africa (printed in bold type) with incomes elsewhere.

COUNTRY OR POPULATION GROUP	INCOME (U.S. $)
Switzerland (1981)	15,698
Germany, Federal Republic of (1982)	10,688
Canada (1982)	10,193
Australia (1980)	9,914
Japan (1982)	8,836[1]
United States of America (1981)	8,827
Libya (1982)	7,900
France (1982)	7,179
United Kingdom (1982)	6,309[2]
White South Africans (1980)	5,797
Germany, Democratic Republic of (1979)	5,340
Hong Kong (1982)	4,952
Greece (1980)	4,590
Union of Soviet Socialist Republics (1979)	4,402[1]
Gabon (1981)	2,974
Taiwan (1981)	2,570[1]
Brazil (1981)	2,370[2]
Chile (1982)	2,178[2]
Mexico (1982)	2,158
Algeria (1982)	1,951

(CONTINUED ON NEXT PAGE.)

SOURCES: Figures for United States and U.S.S.R. from *Statistical Abstract of the United States, 1982-83*. Other country figures from U.S. Department of State, *Background Notes*. South African population group figures from South Africa Foundation.

Country or Population Group	Income (U.S. $)
Asian South Africans (1980)	1,835
Namibia (South West Africa) (1980)	1,695[2]
South Korea (1982)	1,680[1]
All South Africans (1980)[3]	1,528
Black South Africans, Johannesburg Area (1980)	1,408
Colored South Africans (1980)	1,323
Turkey (1981)	1,300
Ivory Coast (1981)	1,153
Botswana (1982)	1,067
Nigeria (1980)	750[2]
All Black South Africans (1980)	623
Niger (1981)	475
Ghana (1980)	420
Sudan (1982)	370
Lesotho (1979)	355
Black South Africans, Homelands (1980)	334
Gambia, The (1981)	330
Senegal (1980)	330[1]
Togo (1978)	319
China, People's Republic of (1982)	298[1]
Guinea (1980)	293
Zambia (1979)	258
Rwanda (1982)	250
India (1982)	245
Tanzania (1982)	240
Mozambique (1980)	220
Malawi (1980)	200[1]
Kenya (1981)	196
Mali (1980)	190
Guinea-Bissau (1979)	170
Zaire (1982)	128[1]

Notes
   1. Gross National Product per capita.
   2. Gross Domestic Product per capita.
   3. According to the *Race Relations Survey, 1984*, household incomes in South Africa broke down like this: *in 1980*—whites, $14,008; Asians, $7,756; coloreds, $5,284; blacks, $2,089; *in 1981*—whites, $15,513; Asians, $8,084; coloreds, $5,704; blacks, $2,380.

The Sullivan Principles

This code of conduct for U.S. firms in South Africa was formulated by Leon Sullivan, a Baptist minister and civil-rights activist, and published in the expanded form below in July 1978.

PRINCIPLE I: Non-segregation of the races in all eating, comfort, and work facilities.
Each signator of the Statement of Principles will proceed immediately to:
• Eliminate all vestiges of racial discrimination.
• Remove all race designation signs.
• Desegregate all eating, comfort, and work facilities.

PRINCIPLE II: Equal and fair employment practices for all employees.
Each signator of the Statement of Principles will proceed immediately to:
• Implement equal and fair terms and conditions of employment.
• Provide non-discriminatory eligibility for benefit plans.
• Establish an appropriate comprehensive procedure for handling and resolving individual employee complaints.
• Support the elimination of all industrial racial discriminatory laws which impede the implementation of equal and fair terms and conditions of employment, such as abolition of job reservations, job fragmentation, and apprenticeship restrictions for blacks and other non-whites.
• Support the elimination of discrimination against the rights of blacks to form or belong to government-registered unions, and acknowledge generally the right of black workers to form their own union or be represented by trade unions where unions already exist.

PRINCIPLE III: Equal pay for all employees doing equal or comparable work for the same period of time.
Each signator of the Statement of Principles will proceed immediately to:
• Design and implement a wage and salary administration plan which is applied equally to all employees regardless of race who are performing equal or comparable work.
• Ensure an equitable system of job classifications, including a review of the distinction between hourly and salaried classifications.
• Determine whether upgrading of personnel and/or jobs in the lower echelons is needed, and if so, implement programs to accomplish this objective expeditiously.

SOURCE: Richard E. Bissell, *South Africa and the United States: The Erosion of an Influence Relationship* (Praeger, 1982).

● Assign equitable wage and salary ranges, the minimum of these to be well above the appropriate local minimum economic living level.

PRINCIPLE IV: Initiation of and development of training programs that will prepare, in substantial numbers, blacks and other non-whites for supervisory, administrative, clerical and technical jobs.

Each signator of the Statement of Principles will proceed immediately to:

● Determine employee training needs and capabilities, and identify employees with potential for further advancement.

● Take advantage of existing outside training resources and activities, such as exchange programs, technical colleges, vocational schools, continuation classes, supervisory courses and similar institutions or programs.

● Support the development of outside training facilities individually or collectively, including technical centers, professional training exposure, correspondence and extension courses, as appropriate, for extensive training outreach.

● Initiate and expand inside training programs and facilities.

PRINCIPLE V: Increasing the number of blacks and other non-whites in management and supervisory positions.

Each signator of the Statement of Principles will proceed immediately to:

● Identify, actively recruit, train, and develop a sufficient and significant number of blacks and other non-whites to assure that as quickly as possible there will be appropriate representation of blacks and other non-whites in the management group of each company.

● Establish management development programs for blacks and other non-whites, as appropriate, and improve existing programs and facilities for developing management skills of blacks and other non-whites.

● Identify and channel high-management-potential blacks and other non-white employees into management-development programs.

PRINCIPLE VI: Improving the quality of employees' lives outside the work environment in such areas as housing, transportation, schooling, recreation and health facilities.

● Evaluate existing and/or develop programs, as appropriate, to address the specific needs of black and other non-white employees in the areas of housing, health care, transportation, and recreation.

● Evaluate methods of utilizing existing, expanded, or newly established in-house medical facilities or other medical programs to improve medical care of all non-whites and their dependents.

● Participate in the development of programs that address the educational needs of employees, their dependents and the local community. Both individual and collective programs should be considered, including such activities as literary education, business training, direct assistance to local schools, contributions, and scholarships.

● With all the foregoing in mind, it is the objective of the companies to involve and assist in the education and training of large and telling numbers of blacks and other non-whites as quickly as possible. The ultimate impact of this effort is intended to be of massive proportion, reaching millions.

Sullivan Principles: Signatory Companies

The U.S. companies listed here had signed the Sullivan code of conduct for business operations in South Africa as of January 3, 1984.

AFIA Worldwide Insurance
Abbott Laboratories
American Cyanamid Company
American Express Company
American Home Products Corporation
American Hospital Supply Corporation
American International Group, Inc.
Armco Inc.
Ashland Oil, Inc.

Borden, Inc.
Borg-Warner Corporation
Bristol-Myers Company
Burroughs Corporation
Butterick Company, Inc.

CBS, Inc.
CIGNA Corporation
CPC International, Inc.
Caltex Petroleum Corporation
Carnation Company
Carrier Corporation
J. I. Case Corporation
Caterpillar Tractor Company
Celanese Corporation
The Chase Manhattan Corporation
Chicago Bridge & Iron Company
Citicorp
The Cola-Cola Company
Colgate-Palmolive Company
Control Data Corporation
Cooper Industries, Inc.
Cummins Engine Company, Inc.

D'Arcy MacManus & Masius
   Worldwide, Inc.
Dart & Kraft, Inc.
Deere & Company
Del Monte Corporation
Deloitte Haskins & Sells
Dominion Textile Inc.
Donaldson Company, Inc.
The Dow Chemical Company
E.I. DuPont de Nemours & Company

The East Asiatic Company (S.A.)
   (Pty) Ltd.
Eastman Kodak Company
Eaton Corporation
Englehard Corporation
Exxon Corporation

FMC Corporation
Federal-Mogul Corporation
Ferro Corporation
The Firestone Tire & Rubber Co.
John Fluke Manufacturing Co., Inc.
Fluor Corporation
Ford Motor Company
Franklin Electric Company, Inc.

General Electric Company
General Motors Corporation
The Gillette Company
Goodyear Tire & Rubber Company
W. R. Grace & Company

SOURCE: *Meeting the Mandate for Change,* A Progress Report on the Application of the Sullivan Principles by U.S. Companies in South Africa (New York: Industry Support Unit, 1984).

Walter E. Heller International Corp.
Heublein, Inc.
Hewlett-Packard Company
Honeywell Inc.
Hoover Company
Hyster Company

International Business Machines Corp.
International Harvester Company
International Minerals & Chemicals
    Corporation
International Telephone & Telegraph
    Corporation
The Interpublic Group of Companies,
    Inc.

Johnson Controls, Inc.
Johnson & Johnson
Joy Manufacturing Company

Kellogg Company

Eli Lilly and Company

Marriott Corporation
Marsh & McLennan Companies
Masonite Corporation
McGraw-Hill, Inc.
Measurex Corporation
Merck & Co., Inc.
Mine Safety Appliances Company
Minnesota Mining & Manufacturing
    Company
Mobil Oil Corporation
Monsanto Company
Motorola, Inc.

NCNB Corporation
NCR Corporation
Nabisco Brands Inc.
Nalco Chemical Company
Norton Company
Norton Simon, Inc. (Avis, Inc.)

Olin Corporation
Oshkosh Truck Corporation
Otis Elevator Company

The Parker Pen Company
Pfizer, Inc.
Phelps Dodge Corporation
Phibro-Salomon, Inc.
Phillips Petroleum Company

The Reader's Digest Association, Inc.
Rexnord Inc.
[R.J. Reynolds Industries, Inc.]—see
    Del Monte Corporation and
    Heublein, Inc.
Richardson-Vicks Inc.
Rohm and Haas Corporation

Schering-Plough Corporation
Sentry Insurance—A Mutual Co.
SmithKline Beckman Corporation
Sperry Corporation
Squibb Corporation
[Standard Oil Company of
    California]—see Caltex Petroleum
    Corporation
The Standard Oil Company (Ohio)
The Stanley Works
Sterling Drug Inc.

Tampax Incorporated
[Tenneco, Inc.]—see J. I. Case Corp.
[Texaco Incorporated]—see Caltex
    Petroleum Corporation
J. Walter Thompson Company
Time Incorporated
The Trane Company

Union Carbide Corporation
[United Technologies Corporation]—
    see Carrier Corporation and Otis
    Elevator Company
The Upjohn Company

Warner Communications, Inc.
Warner-Lambert Company
Westinghouse Electric Corporation
Wilbur-Ellis Company

Xerox Corporation

Religious Affiliation in South Africa

1. Blacks

RELIGIOUS BODY OR CATEGORY	ADHERENTS		
	Urban	Non-Urban	Total
Nederduitse Gereformeerd	376,200	727,360	1,103,560
Black independent churches	1,933,300	3,021,800	4,954,000
Lutheran	298,500	399,900	698,400
Anglican	451,720	345,320	797,040
Methodist	841,540	712,740	1,554,280
Presbyterian	182,500	178,120	360,620
Roman Catholic	712,480	964,200	1,676,680
Apostolic Faith Mission	39,720	85,960	125,680
Other Christian churches	498,780	567,400	1,066,180
Congregational	91,680	16,700	208,380
Other non-Christian churches	35,000	66,700	101,700
No religion or objection to state religion ...	1,019,340	3,257,900	4,277,240
TOTAL	6,479,660	10,444,100	16,923,760

2. Whites

RELIGIOUS BODY OR CATEGORY	ADHERENTS		
	Urban	Non-Urban	Total
Nederduitse Gereformeerd	1,414,920	278,720	1,693,640
Gereformeerd	104,940	23,420	128,360
Nederduitsch Hervormd	200,320	46,020	246,340
Anglican	424,940	31,080	456,020
Methodist	386,040	28,040	414,080
Presbyterian	120,820	8,100	128,920
Roman Catholic	375,380	18,260	393,640
Apostolic Faith Mission	109,900	16,020	125,920
Other Christian churches	514,340	52,300	566,640
Jewish/Hebrew	118,380	840	119,220
Other non-Christian churches	25,460	1,580	27,040
No religion or objection to state religion ...	206,560	21,720	228,280
TOTAL	4,002,000	526,100	4,258,100

3. Coloreds

RELIGIOUS BODY OR CATEGORY	ADHERENTS		
	Urban	Non-Urban	Total
Nederduitse Gereformeerd	376,960	301,420	678,380
Black independent churches	87,240	31,100	118,340
Lutheran	60,000	35,640	95,640
Anglican	308,900	42,580	351,480
Methodist	108,360	31,760	140,120
Congregational	131,800	38,220	170,020
Roman Catholic	228,660	36,160	264,820
Apostolic Faith Mission	36,060	12,800	48,860
Other Christian churches	360,200	46,280	406,480
Islam	162,900	800	163,700
Other non-Christian churches	27,260	3,100	30,360
No religion or objection to state religion	113,960	30,620	144,580
TOTAL	2,002,300	610,480	2,612,780

4. Asians

RELIGIOUS BODY OR CATEGORY	ADHERENTS		
	Urban	Non-Urban	Total
Afrikaans churches	3,500	440	3,940
Hindu	457,980	54,380	512,360
Lutheran	920	220	1,140
Anglican	8,440	460	8,900
Methodist	3,700	620	4,320
Presbyterian	1,760	140	1,900
Roman Catholic	19,960	1,200	21,160
Full Gospel	20,460	2,380	22,840
Other Christian churches	33,880	4,420	38,300
Islam	148,420	5,880	154,300
Other non-Christian churches	11,380	840	12,220
No religion or objection to state religion	33,420	6,540	39,960
TOTAL	743,820	77,500	821,320

SOURCE: *South Africa 1984*, chapter 44 (Johannesburg: Chris van Rensburg Publications, 1984). Figures based on 5 per cent sample of 1980 census.

South African Churches in Ecumenical Councils

South African Council of Churches

MEMBER CHURCHES

African Catholic Church
African Methodist Episcopal Church
African Orthodox Church
Bantu Presbyterian Church
Christian New Salem Church
Church of the Province of South Africa
Evangelical Lutheran Church
Methodist Church of Southern Africa
Moravian Church
National Baptist Council of South Africa
Nederduitse Gereformeerde Kerk in Africa
Religious Society of Friends
Salvation Army
Tsonga Presbyterian Church
United Evangelical Lutheran Church
  of Southwest Africa

MEMBER ORGANIZATIONS

Apostolic Ministers Association
Black Community Programs
Christian Institute of South Africa
Edendale Lay Ecumenical Center
Federation of Pentecostal Apostolic
  Mission Churches in South Africa
Interdenominational African Ministers
  Association
Reformed Independent Churches Assoc.
Wilgespruit Fellowship Center
Young Women's Christian Association

OBSERVER CHURCHES

Evangelical Lutheran Churches (Transvaal)
Nederduitse Gereformeerde Sendingkerk
Reformed Church in Africa
Roman Catholic Church

World Council of Churches

Bantu Presbyterian Church
Church of the Province of South Africa
Evangelical Lutheran Church
Methodist Church of Southern Africa
Moravian Church

Presbyterian Church of Africa
Presbyterian Church of Southern Africa
United Congregational Church
  of Southern Africa

World Alliance of Reformed Churches

Evangelical Presbyterian Church
Nederduitse Gereformeerde Kerk (NGK)
  (*membership suspended, August 1982*)
Nederduitse Gereformeerde Kerk in Africa
Presbyterian Church of Southern Africa

Reformed Church in Africa
Reformed Presbyterian Church
  in Southern Africa
United Congregational Church
  of Southern Africa

(The Nederduitse Hervormde Kerk in Africa withdrew its membership from the WARC in September 1982.)

Current Issues Facing American Corporations in South Africa

This report (excerpted here) of a symposium held in September 1981 appeared in the February 1982 issue of "The Corporate Examiner," a monthly newsletter of the Interfaith Center on Corporate Responsibility (ICCR). The sections in italics are by the editor of the report.

Introduction. *On September 15, 1981, approximately 125 participants and observers, representing twenty-nine Fortune 500 companies and thirty churches and religious communities, met for a full day's discussion of corporate policies on South Africa. Though all declared their abhorrence of South Africa's apartheid system, there was considerable difference of opinion about effective strategies for change in South Africa as well as what constitutes meaningful change. Organized in cooperation with General Motors Corporation and Ford Motor Company, the symposium was sponsored by church organizations. The dialogue, held at the International House in New York City and chaired by former United Nations Ambassador Donald McHenry, consisted of three panels: "Corporate Performance in the Workplace," "U.S. Investors and the South African Government," and "How Corporations Can Contribute to Meaningful Social Change in South Africa."*

Following are excerpts from several of the statements made by church and corporate spokespersons. The excerpts were selected by J. Brian Sheehan, Ph.D., a social anthropologist and 1982 University of Minnesota International Human Rights Fellow who is working at ICCR. Dr. Sheehan also wrote the transitional narrative and analysis found with the excerpts.

Robert McCabe of General Motors *spoke first during the introductory session. GM employs over 5,400 people in South Africa, primarily in the Port Elizabeth area. Mr. McCabe stated that GM believed maintaining the status quo in South Africa was not satisfactory. Further, he added that the corporation and board of directors:*

. . . are convinced that by our presence and adherence to sound and reasoned operating principles, we have the opportunity to be a positive force for change in that government's apartheid policies. [If] we give up on the prospects for significant and peaceful change and abandon the black and other non-white peoples of that country, their only course of action to get relief from racial oppression would be violent revolution. We believe that those who advocate withdrawal before exhausting all peaceful alternatives which have the potential to contribute to change, are not pursuing the best interests of the blacks and other non-whites in that country. . . .

Mr. McCabe went on to elaborate on how GM worked for social change in South Africa:

GMSA's policies provide for equal pay, regardless of race, for all employees with comparable seniority who do similar work in the same job classification.

As of June 30 of this year, GMSA's hourly work force was 20 per cent white, 54 per cent colored, and 26 per cent black and included 143 non-white supervisors. There were 63 colored and 24 black salaried employees.

General Motors South African has been a leader in developing and implementing programs to improve conditions for non-whites in South Africa, and we have aggressively pursued the objectives of equal opportunity for all of our employees in that country. A major example of this effort is our early endorsement of Dr. Sullivan's "Statement of Principles of U.S. Firms with Affiliates in . . . South Africa."

McCabe went on to discuss some of the dilemmas faced by a company, which though formally committed to implementation of principles of social justice, continues to do business in an apartheid system. He explained GM's position on . . . the sale of goods to the South African police and military:

. . . The U.S. Department of Commerce issued a bulletin February 1978, which imposed an embargo on the export or reexport of U.S.-origin commodities and technical data to the South African police and military.

In response to this regulation, GM implemented several measures to assure our compliance. These range from a comprehensive review of all of our vehicles and parts containing any content or technology of U.S. origin, to the complete exclusion of any vehicles with U.S. content or technology from all quotations and tenders to South African miitary or police entities.

GMSA's total sales to the South African government have declined sharply in recent years. GM continuously monitors its marketing activities in South Africa to assure adherence to the Department of Commerce regulations.

Certain stockholders have expressed concern regarding the ethical and social implications of GM continuing such sales and have proposed that the corporation go well beyond the compliance with U.S. regulations and discontinue all sales to the police and military entities in South Africa. GM, however, believes that cessation of these sales, which are nominal and provide no special capabilities to the military or police, could cause our subsidiary to lose not only a large portion of its already reduced business with the government, but that we would also lose significant non-government business.

Accordingly, it is our position that discontinuation of such sales would seriously threaten the capability of the corporation to continue operations in South Africa and thereby eliminate the opportunity to contribute and promote needed change in that country. Additionally, the refusal of GMSA to sell vehicles without U.S. content and technology to the South African police and military would not affect the operations of those agencies.

The State Department has indicated that sales by a U.S. subsidiary of non-U.S.-origin commodities and technical data to the South African police and military are not affected by U.S. law and that the United States has not made it a policy objective to keep such commodities and technical data from reaching the South African military and police. . . .

It has long been GM's belief that the corporation cannot effectively promote the necessary social and economic changes in South Africa if it withdraws from the country. GM believes it has played a part in improving the economic and living conditions for its non-white employees and their families, and that GMSA's methods of doing business continue to be a constructive force that has brought social equality closer to reality.

In a second keynote address, **William P. Thompson, stated clerk of the United Presbyterian Church in the U.S.A.,** *reaffirmed the churches' unyielding opposition to apartheid and discussed the concerns of church investors about U.S. corporate investment in South Arica:*

I am particularly pleased that Mr. McCabe is here from General Motors. I have had very profitable discussions with the recently retired chairman of General Motors, Mr. Tom Murphy, particularly centering on the issue of the sale of the products of General Motors South African to the police and military. The conversations have been mutually instructive but I regret to say that the policies which Mr. McCabe has outlined are exactly the same that Mr. Murphy conveyed to me some four or five years ago. And so we begin at about the point where I began my conversation with Mr. Murphy.

The system of apartheid as practiced in South Africa is an affront to the religious, moral, and ethical convictions of the churches, the United Nations, and the world. Apartheid as a system has economic, political, social, and cultural ramifications expressed in a multitude of discriminatory laws and practices. It, however, involves a more basic issue because it violates the meaning of creation, the very nature and destiny of all humanity. Apartheid embodies a pattern of injustice and oppression imposed on a people solely because of their race. It involves a denial of inherent claims of all people to dignity, equality, and freedom. It borders on the denial of even the right to life itself. In a religious sense, it involves the breaking of the fellowship of those who believe in God as the creator of all people. The churches hold that same conviction today.

Our fear, as church investors and, indeed, as concerned Americans, is that the United States companies are being drawn into one side of a racial conflict—a side which we are confident is the wrong side. It is the duty of the churches to seek out and to speak out for justice in an unjust world, and the churches will not be confused by laws that permit, enforce, or allow collaboration with blatant oppression. We are here today from the churches in part to pledge that we will not be sidetracked from our support of our brothers and sisters in South Africa.

I. CORPORATE PERFORMANCE IN THE WORKPLACE

Dan Purnell, executive director of the International Council for Equality of Opportunity Principles, Inc., *was the first speaker on the first symposium panel. The International Council for Equality of Opportunity Principles, the organization founded by the Rev. Leon Sullivan, monitors and reports regularly on the performance of the U.S. companies operating in South Africa which have signed the Sullivan Principles on employment practices in South Africa. Mr. Purnell said that during a trip to South Africa from which he had only just returned, he had talked to people "on the streets, in* *their homes, in the factories, and everywhere." According to Mr. Purnell, people said that the Sullivan Principles had made a profound difference in their lives. Though he believes they need to do more, Mr. Purnell stated, "American companies who are working in South Africa are the most viable vehicle for changing that republic."*

Purnell was followed by **Robert Copp, manager of the International Labor Office of the Ford Motor Company.** *In his remarks, Mr. Copp made reference to the Wiehahn Commission, the first of two commissions established by the South African government in the aftermath of the township uprisings. The commission, under the leadership of Professor Nicholas Wiehahn, studied South African labor laws affecting black workers and was charged with making recommendations for "the adjustment of the existing system." Mr. Copp discussed Ford's experiences with black trade unions:*

The Wiehahn Commission has been making an effort to assure at least equal treatment for trade unions with black members. During the days when trade unions with black members were not eligible for registration and, therefore, formal recognition in the labor-relations system of South Africa, Ford of South Africa was approached by a group of its black employees who had organized themselves as the UAW [United Auto Workers]. Actually they had been organized with sponsorship from a recognized, registered colored union, the Motor Assembly and Rubber Workers of South Africa, and with outside assistance from the UAW in the United States and from the International Metal Workers Federation in Geneva, but it was not a registered, formal, legal organization. And Ford, in late 1976, was faced with the question of how to deal with this body of employees.

The demonstrable majority representation required a certain skirting of the law in that the Industrial Conciliation Act and the Black Labor Administration Act did not permit the check-off of union dues. With the advice of South African legal counsel, Ford South Africa developed the idea of accepting, as a demonstration of interest in this unregistered union organization, a check-off for a subscription to the union's burial insurance fund. When 50 per cent plus one of these subscriptions had been presented to the company's management, Ford South Africa recognized the unregistered UAW as a representative of its black employees. That was in March 1977, almost concurrently with the drafting of the Sullivan Principles. Meantime, under amendments to the Industrial Conciliation Act, which followed the Wiehahn Commission recommendations, the original unregistered UAW has merged into and become a part of the already registered multi-racial, basically colored union. So where we are today is formal, black participation in the legal labor-relations system through that registered union.

Dr. Avery Post, president of the United Church of Christ, *raised the question in his presentation of whether or not the Sullivan Principles had been coopted. Post quoted one South African who referred to the Sullivan Principles as "polish" on his chains:*

From the churches' perspective, the U.S. corporation cannot be in South Africa without keeping the door open to not being there at all. The general principle is that the good we try to do can be and is often coopted by the powers of evil. That principle in our view has to be part of the calculus used by corporation policy-makers in relation to the total South African situation, including the workplace.

I suppose that some of us have to observe openly and publicly that we have some concerns about the value of the Sullivan Principles, that they too have been coopted. "These principles," said one South African person, "attempt to polish my chains and make them more comfortable. I want to cut my chains and cast them away." I think the Sullivan Principles remind us that our good works are always becoming less than we intend because of the pride with which we stroke them. From a perspective of the church, the workplace is a significant arena of access to justice for persons to whom justice has been denied and also access to the fearsome issues of destiny that lie ahead for South Africa.

In the question-and-answer period following this panel, a church representative characterized South Africa as "a country in flame" and questioned the efficacy of the Sullivan Principles. Declaring "I submit to you that as each black leader becomes a person of power and influence for the majority, he is systematically picked off and jailed," the church representative expressed grave doubts on the possibility of peaceful change in South Africa.

II. U.S. INVESTORS AND THE SOUTH AFRICAN GOVERNMENT

In the second panel, **Roger Wheeler of Control Data Corporation** *discussed his company's South African operations. He said that, in contrast to its procedures in other countries, Control Data asked its salesmen in South Africa to be selective in their choice of customers so that Control Data products would not be used for repressive purposes. Wheeler also said that management in Control Data headquarters in Minneapolis–St. Paul reviewed what the machines were to be used for before installation in South Africa.*

In a strong statement, **Regina Murphy, S.C., of the Sisters of Charity of St. Vincent de Paul** *criticized current U.S. business operations in South Africa as approximating a partnership with the South African regime in its enforcement of apartheid:*

The question of corporate relations with the South African government has been an item of central concern for the churches over the past decade and more. We fear that the record shows a comfortable commercial relationship, one in which many United States companies have sold strategic products and technological skills which assist the South African government in administering and strengthening that apparatus of apartheid. Sanctioning sales to the police and military is one of the clearest examples of the ways in which United States companies collaborate with the South African government in maintaining white supremacy. General Motors and Ford continue to sell vehicles to the South African police and military despite the United States embargo regulations. The fact is that while the letter of the law is being observed, the spirit certainly is not.

We believe that direct sales of this sort to the police and military provide unequivocal backing for the forces of violence and repression. General Motors', Ford's, and Mobil's claim to be a positive force in South Africa seems, in many cases, unfortunately to be a cruel joke when viewed in the context of the entire situation and in the context of sales to the police and military.

Another example of strategic sales to the South African government is the sale of computers. Our major computer companies, IBM, Control Data, Burroughs, Hewlett-

Packard and so on, are all active in South Africa, active in selling directly to the government or to the parastatal agencies which are part of that government. The United States computers are found in the National Institute of Telecommunications Research, the Electricity Supply Commission, the Atomic Energy Board, the South African Airways, South Africa Railways, and so on. As a result they enable the government to do its business, carry out its communications, transportation, and to administer and maintain apartheid.

In short American computers enable the infrastructures of the apartheid government to be maintained. Commendable as the policies of Control Data, Burroughs, IBM, Ford and General Motors are, the results of policies that forbid sales abridging human rights have not been as commendable. South African agencies are filled with U.S. computers, making apartheid function that much more efficiently.

Another area of concern for the churches as we view corporate relations with the South African government, is the necessary compliance with South African laws. The Official Secrets Act prevents U.S. oil companies from knowing who their clients are or how much of their product is sold to the police and military. Recently reaffirmed Key Points Legislation allows armed militia to be stationed on the company premises of strategic industries and plants to be "secured."

These and other examples cause many of us in the church to believe that the United States companies are in a commercial partnership with the South African government. A partnership which, while unintentional, provides concrete assistance to that government as it pursues its apartheid policies. We call on business today to make its voice heard louder and clearer in opposition to the apartheid policies and practices of the South African government and to voice that opposition in actions as well as words.

Following Sister Regina's remarks, **Timothy H. Smith, ICCR's executive director,** *posed the question:*

What happens in the context of increasing militarization when our companies are forced to do things that they should refuse to do, in conscience, or that they wouldn't decide to do here [in the United States]? We see the situation [in South Africa] becoming increasingly militarized; we see our companies being caught up in that and being put in a very difficult position indeed. It troubles us greatly.

Netx, **Marc Sussman, a representative of Chemical Bank,** *read the bank's official policy concerning loans to South Africa:*

As a matter of firm policy, we make no loans or other credit accommodations whatsoever to the government of South Africa or any of its instrumentalities or political subdivisions. The bank has no intention of doing so until the question of apartheid is resolved. This has been our standing policy since 1974. In the private sector we do have short-term trade-related transactions involving non-strategic goods.

The Rev. M. William Howard, Jr., then president of the National Council of Churches of Christ in the U.S.A., *explained the NCC's opposition to foreign bank loans to South Africa:*

In a nutshell it is our position that foreign bank loans to South Africa act to strengthen apartheid and white minority rule. Whatever the intention or desire of the lender, the South African regime uses such loans to bolster its position and to resist demands for a change from outside and inside.

Although a number of banks tried to legitimatize their lending by making loans of a "socially productive nature," it is clear that this was merely an attempt to keep this channel of finance open while attempting to silence critics. The willingness of foreign banks to be publicly associated with South Africa again has tremendous economic and political significance for the apartheid regime.

One reason for the demand [for loans] is the cost of financing an increasingly militaristic state that is faced with the prospects of international sanctions. As Owen Horwood, South Africa's finance minister, stated when announcing the [September 1980, $250 million] loan [to the South African Ministry of Finance from an international consortium including Citibank], "We did not really need the money, but it is important to fly our flag in the international capital markets."

Thus Citibank assisted in building South Africa's moral and financial credibility as well as providing hard cash for apartheid. The response to Citibank has been direct and clear. Tens of millions of dollars of church accounts have been withdrawn.

Bill Kopliwitz of Citibank *responded to Mr. Howard's remarks by stating that banks, corporations—the American business community—were in South Africa essentially to conduct business. Kopliwitz, who characterized the South African system as evil, justified Citibank's loan on the ground that it ". . . will increase the skills, the welfare, the capacity of blacks in South Africa to look after their affairs and to promote the social change that we have been talking about."*

III. HOW CORPORATIONS CAN CONTRIBUTE TO MEANINGFUL SOCIAL CHANGE IN SOUTH AFRICA

The third panel was begun by **Dr. David Preus, president of the American Lutheran Church,** *who called on American corporations to support the just aspirations of the South African majority by making no new investments in South Africa and by bringing pressure on the South African government.*

We ask you as a general rule to make no new investments in South Africa. We also ask you to reorder the allocation of your assets in South Africa, material and human, in such fashion that the overarching objective of all your operations there addresses black economic, educational, and social progress as well as providing necessary goods and services. We believe you can do this and also earn a suitable return on your investment. Without directly entering the political process, corporate executives can, in personal dialogue, implant and strengthen the concepts of justice and equality through universal political opportunity.

Bill Broderick, director of research and analysis for International Government Affairs at the Ford Motor Company, *stated that whether meaningful social change was possible in South Africa was a legitimate question. Broderick stated that the two prerequisites for successful social change were a strong and articulated commitment from U.S. management and an imaginative and determined implementation at the local level. Broderick stated that he felt U.S. companies could work for change in the workplace and the community in the areas of housing, education and training.*

Next **Father Charles Dahm, O.P., a Dominican priest from Chicago,** *both raised and answered negatively the question of whether U.S. companies can effect meaningful* *social change in South Africa. In his remarks, Fr. Dahm mentions the Wiehahn Commission, discussed by an earlier speaker, and the Riekert Commission, the second of the government commissions established after the township uprisings. The Riekert Commission, charged with the study of manpower utilization, in May 1979 recommended, with some adjustments, the continuation of the influx-control and the pass-law systems, the backbone of South Africa's program of separate development. Fr. Dahm stated:*

I think one of the key points is in the title of our panel and that is "meaningful social change." Bishop Desmond Tutu's remark that we've seen "some improvement" but we haven't seen any "social change" is very relevant.

What is the cost? While these few benefits are occurring, brought about by rather courageous people who are willing to stick their necks out in South Africa, it's our position that the cost is tremendous.

I'll just cite briefly some of those. One is [that in South Africa] we have a stronger state apparatus than ever before. The military has become largely self-sufficient, producing arms itself. Economically the country is much stronger and self-sufficient than it ever was.

Two, there is a sustained and strengthened policy and program for separate development.

The third point is where we might say there has been a little bit of social change in the Wiehahn Commission recommendations and, to a much lesser extent, the Riekert Commission recommendations. We have some recognition of black trade unions, but we know that registration is practically at the discretion of the Ministry of Labor. Take the Riekert Commission: the residency requirements to give blacks residency rights are practically cynical. They're almost impossible to fulfill for any significant number of black people.

Number four, the gap between black and white wages: the data I have indicate that the gap between white and black wages is worse.

A fifth area, with regard to social change: what we have seen is a growing likelihood of a violent uprising.

Sixthly, strengthening in the hard-line position among the leaders of the country: Are we seeing them weaken in their position or is it actually getting stronger? My reading of the situation is that they're actually digging in.

Number seven, is there any evidence of political power-sharing? We've had the explicit denial of that. There will never be one person, one vote.

Eighth and finally, the repression against freedom of speech has only increased, not decreased, in the last decade.

Enlarging upon Fr. Dahm's comments, Mr. Smith, ICCR's director stated:

My final point would echo one I made earlier. Where do U.S. companies stand as violence unfolds? Will our company technology, our personnel, our Mobil oil, our GM and Ford trucks and cars be used by the South African government as they try to keep power? Will our companies be caught up in supporting and interpreting positively what the South African government is doing as it tries to maintain control? I would hope not, but again I think the record has not been such that allows us to sit by comfortably.

APPENDIX G

Revolution, Sayeth the Churchman; One Soul at a Time, Says a Businessman

In this article, published in the February 6, 1978, issue of the business biweekly magazine "Forbes," Robert J. Flaherty gives excerpts from a discussion between three executives of a U.S. corporation with operations in South Africa and three churchmen.

TO THOSE ACCUSTOMED to seeing issues in black and white—no pun intended—South Africa is a simple issue—injustice—and there is a simple solution: turn over power to representatives of the black majority. But is the issue that simple? What of the rights of the four million whites, many of whose ancestors have lived in South Africa for three centuries? And what of the undisputed fact that the blacks of white-ruled South Africa are decades ahead of their cousins in black-ruled Africa in education, in income, in job opportunities?

Americans of the liberal persuasion and many churchmen have demanded that American business pull out of South Africa as a means of helping bring down the white government and bringing a black group to power. Polaroid Corp. has pulled out of South Africa. But other American companies hang on, many of them pledged to make extra efforts on behalf of the black people they employ.

Last December [1977] William Norris, the founder and chairman of Control Data Corp. of Minneapolis, found himself smack in the middle of the controversy. With two aides he journeyed to his New York offices. There he confronted a group of prominent churchmen who were seeking to pressure American business to cease operating in South Africa. Norris hoped to persuade them that his company's presence was a blessing to the blacks and in no way represented approval of the Afrikaner government.

This was no clear-cut argument between the forces of God and forces of Mammon. Norris, 66, a computer pioneer, an electrical engineer by profession, is a thoughtful man concerned with the moral issues of the day. He and his company have been active in finding jobs for unemployed young people, especially blacks.

But in the two-hour discussion the two sides ended up farther apart than they had started. The whole thing was a fascinating demonstration of how two groups, each equally sincere, can look at the same problem and come up with totally opposed courses of action. The churchmen, surprisingly, took an intellectual point of view—seemingly more interested in abstract principles of justice than in the fate of a few individuals. For his part, Norris did not fall back on the argument that "business is business" but put forward a moral argument for his firm's staying in the country.

The participants in the discussion were:

124

From Control Data: WILLIAM C. NORRIS, chairman; NORBERT R. BERG, senior vice president for administration and personnel; and GARY H. LOHN, vice president for human resource development and public affairs.

From church bodies: WILLIAM P. THOMPSON, president of the National Council of Churches of Christ in the U.S.A. and stated clerk of the General Assembly of the United Presbyterian Church; TIMOTHY H. SMITH, director of the Interfaith Center on Corporate Responsibility; and FRANK P. WHITE, a founder of the Interfaith Center on Corporate Responsibility and a staff aide in the United Presbyterian Church.

Excerpts appear below.

THOMPSON: The United Presbyterian Church has long been concerned about the developing repression in South Africa. The National Council of Churches and the World Council of Churches have expressed similar concerns. The United Presbyterian Church has come reluctantly to the view that the situation as it now exists in South Africa is not likely to improve by persuasion, and therefore continued economic participation in, and support of, the present regime in South Africa is truly counterproductive in bringing about any improvement in the situation.

NORRIS: You mean you see no change in the past year?

THOMPSON: Yes. But it has been a change for the worse. The plight of the blacks is deteriorating progressively.

NORRIS: There has been some small improvement in the economic situation of the blacks. Employment is slowly increasing, and to me a job is fundamental. In our own experience there, it's a bit easier for us to hire blacks now; it's a little bit easier to provide job training; there's definitely more interest in computer-based education. To me that's progress, and having observed how slowly things change, it's somewhat encouraging.

THOMPSON: The black people within the churches that we have contact with would not be as optimistic as you people are. They feel that the denial of their participation in the decision-making processes of the country is hardly compensated for by some slight improvement in economic status. The recent banning of every liberal organization in the country, the continued arrest of any black leaders whom the government considers to be dangerous, the death of Steve Biko are further signs of a progressively totalitarian regime.

The white people in power are giving greater evidence of an extreme defensive posture that is being expressed by increasingly repressive measures toward the blacks and coloreds. I personally find absolutely unacceptable the basic premise on which their society is organized—which is, the blacks are citizens of small enclaves and that as such they are strangers in South Africa, and have no rights.

NORRIS: Well, there's no issue there. A whole litany of countries are based on completely unacceptable premises. For example, we are a lot more careful in Iran about how we use the telephone than we are in South Africa. But we have black employees, 19 out of 190 in South Africa. We faced enormous problems in hiring them. They're iliterate, they're just not equipped. And we have a firm company policy that when we hire somebody, we try to hire only the best. Once they become part of Control Data we have an obligation to provide them with that job for just as long as they do their part. We have a covenant, and I feel just as dedicated to preserving the jobs of those blacks in South Africa, as I—

SMITH (shouting): Mr. Norris, you can't be serious! Nineteen blacks is not a significant employee population in South Africa. It's meaningless in terms of social change.

NORRIS: You and I are not on the same wavelength. One person is significant to me. *One* job. We thought it was significant when we put in the first black custom computer engineer in South Africa—that just hadn't been done. We are talking about overall social change—lighting one candle rather than cursing the darkness. You talk about a man's life, and to me that's important.

SMITH: Your twenty-odd black workers are virtually insignificant in terms of social change in South Africa, but not insignificant in terms of those twenty people's lives.

But let's talk about the withdrawal position. This position is increasingly being held in this country and among the black African nations where you may be trying to do business. The government of Nigeria said they will begin to look at their own business dealings with companies, and if that company is in South Africa, consider that a negative factor in terms of—

NORRIS: A boycott?

SMITH: Perhaps it could be seen in that light, but they see it as saying they prefer that companies not be in South Africa. I'm talking about overall social change, not the little candles in the dark.

The reason we wanted the meeting today as shareholders was that we think the best step Control Data can take at this time is to develop a policy as [Polaroid has, of making no further sales or leasing of equipment to the South African government]. We're convinced that in South Africa today there would be very few sales that could be made to the government that wouldn't contribute to the oppression of the people there.

NORRIS (upset): You're looking for a macrosolution. Like the problem of unemployment, everyone's looking for a macrosolution. There isn't one. We've got to get down to the microlevel and grub for each job and save the job you've got. Speaking of not selling to the government, one of the dedications I have is to bring computer-based education to South Africa. There is no other way that you'll ever close that enormous educational gap in South Africa except through the use of the computer. If I say today that I'm not going to sell the government a computer, then I can't go down there and try to solve that educational problem.

THOMPSON: I would prefer not to have you do it than to do it through that present government.

NORRIS: Why? Don't you want those people to have an education?

THOMPSON: Certainly, but the present government is the greatest obstacle to that. The situation in South Africa today is a revolution. It's being conducted by schoolboys, and they're leaving the country in droves simply because they are being shot down in the streets, and I don't think we're realistic to talk about computer education of young people who are giving their lives in the interest of freedom.

CDC's BERG: I want to make sure I understand your position. You mean if we have the opportunity to sell a computer to the South African government and their computer was going to be used on computer-based education to increase the literacy of the black people and therefore make them more employable, that your preference would be that we not sell that computer?

THOMPSON: Today tens of thousands of school-goers are on strike; the whole school system has ground to a halt. People have started rebelling against the white school system. Remember the debate over the use of Afrikaans as a language in the schools? The demand is: "we must get rid of this education system which is designed to make us become serfs forever." The educational system is intentionally designed to make sure that the black pópulation will never be equal with the white. You're working with the architects of a system that want to keep blacks in an inferior position.

WHITE: There are all kinds of education. Could the government use computer-based education programs to educate the military? What possible kinds of restrictions would be placed on that?

NORRIS: You can't place restrictions on a computer that you put in someone else's country.

SMITH: But if you are concerned about human rights, but can't determine how your computers would be used, isn't the best thing not to sell computers?

NORRIS: Well, then, you wouldn't be selling many computers in this world. You do the best you can, and that's exactly what we're doing. I can sell you toothpicks that are used in the dining room and you can push them in people's eardrums and kill them.

SMITH: I think you people would look really bad if you started that program and word got out that the South African government was using those computers to train police or military.

NORRIS: We don't worry about looking bad. I try to do some good, and if in the process there's some bad, okay, I did the best I could. Black guys standing down around there without any education, trying to make it alone is a pretty sad thing. Right here in New York City it's sad enough. We ought to be talking about New York City instead of South Africa with most of the black kids here without a job. Yes, and it's right here in our backyard, and what are we doing about it? Are we talking about that? No, we're talking about something in South Africa that we can't do very much about.

SMITH: I think we can.

NORRIS: We keep in touch with South Africa too and are as well read on the subject. We aren't going to pull out of South Africa. We have a commitment to 190 employees there. We really believe we are a force for good. We think the best approach is to try to help people to get jobs.

BERG: Norris devotes about a fourth of his time on the jobs issue in the U.S. and that's our approach in South Africa. You can't get people jobs unless they're literate and trained, so we're going after our computer-education program. We'll probably be working with other companies, and I don't really care if we have to do it in some way involved with the South African government. It will help black people achieve some share in the economy. This is a summary of our position.

THOMPSON: I don't want any doubt that we disagree with your policy. As a stockholder we think we have a right to be heard about it.

BERG: We've got 40,000 stockholders. You deserved to hear a recap of our position and you've got it.

THOMPSON: As we look at South Africa right now there's a national rebellion going on. There are people being shot in the streets every day.

NORRIS: Your view on that is quite different from ours. We have people working and living down there who don't see rebellion. Moreover, I can't see where denying the government some computers by some American companies is going to have any effect at all. They can get computers from Japan.

SMITH: No, I think when an IBM or Control Data won't expand or sell to the government it will be a real body blow.

BERG: It just creates the Stalingrad thing where the people [white South Africans] get tougher and tougher and their government is saying: "What the hell are you doing meddling in our internal affairs?"

THOMPSON: You're not meddling; your decisions are your own.

NORRIS: If you advocate withdrawal or some kind of partial boycott, you're in fact adding to the increasing unemployment for the black people there and the social turmoil. In a nutshell—the conditions that foment revolution. Are you advocating revolution?

THOMPSON: There is a revolution going on there now.

BERG: Are you advocating an escalation of that?

THOMPSON: My personal sentiments are with those who are revolting. The people in the streets of Soweto are the George Washingtons of that country. We don't apologize for being on the side of the freedom forces. We've given money and will continue to give assistance to them. I submit that if you are really in favor of long-term social justice in South Africa, Control Data might think about supporting some of the educational needs of the independence movement.

BERG: You have to characterize us as evolutionists.

THOMPSON: I see no hope for evolution in South Africa. The time is past. I am asking you not to support the oppressors which you are now doing despite your pronouncements to the contrary.

NORRIS (very angry with a trembling voice): I take very direct issue with that! Remember the five million Kulaks that Stalin murdered? There's just enough power in South Africa to solve that problem [the Stalin] way [if the whites] choose to. What you're talking about brings them [the whites] closer to that alternative.

THOMPSON: We've listened for twenty years as companies with operations in South Africa said, "Don't lean on us and things will change." But friendly persuasion has not worked, and we've got to start looking at ways of leaning. [South African blacks] are saying things to us such as: "You are trying to polish our chains and make them more comfortable, but instead we want them cast off." They also say, "We have been suffering for a long time, and if the withdrawal of certain foreign concerns occurs we may continue to suffer, but white South Africa will start feeling the pinch too."

BERG: The South African whites today feel generally bitter that the very considerable relaxation of discrimination and the real changes of attitudes have gone unnoticed by the West. Bad news is news, and nothing favorable gets reported. They may well ask what the West has ever done except criticize.

SMITH: I've heard this talk for ten years. When are people finally going to recognize that the level of oppression in South Africa has come to such a stage that we are not going to talk about putting curtains on the windows of the concentration camp any longer? We don't question the motivation of Control Data, but are very skeptical about how that government might use your computers. We'll file a shareholder resolution and then you people take a look at it. . . .

Southern Africa

A Policy Statement by the Governing Board of the National Council of Churches

The statement from which this excerpt was taken was adopted by the NCC Board on November 10, 1977. The section printed here was preceded by a discussion of "theological context," "history," "some specifics of the current situation," and "the rise of liberation movements."

THERE ARE MANY TIES which join the people of the United States to the human crisis in southern Africa. Three of the more important ones are historic, religious, and economic.

(1) HISTORY: The origins of the present conflict in southern Africa can be traced to the early sixteenth century, when European powers, bringing racial, economic, and expansionist policies, established colonies in this area. Some of the same European powers colonized the Americas, introducing a system of slavery which utilized Africans. Some of the slaves came from southern Africa and were exploited in the subsequent economic development of the United States. This fundamental historical link between the United States and southern Africa is too often overlooked.

The long struggle to end slavery in the United States and the subsequent movements of black Americans to acquire civil rights for themselves bear many similarities to the present struggles being waged by the African people in southern Africa. However, the similarities must not obscure the profound difference between the movement for civil rights in the United States and the struggles for liberation in southern Africa. Black Americans have largely struggled for the end of racial discrimination and the right to participate fully in existing political, economic, and social institutions. In contrast, the African people in southern Africa are struggling to end racist minority rule and for fundamental transformation of the institutions in their countries.

(2) CHURCHES: Another fundamental link between the United States and southern Africa is the Church. Some United States churches have maintained missionary activity in southern Africa for more than a century. Missionaries from the United States preached the gospel, and built churches, schools, and hospitals. But they also often abetted the development of white domination. Because of this, the United States churches and the Church at large must share some moral responsibility for the present human crisis in southern Africa.

(3) ECONOMICS: A different kind of link between the United States and southern Africa has been forged by the global reach of the multinational corporations. More than 350 United States–based companies do business in southern Africa. The investment of those companies in southern Africa has greatly increased in the last decades. The main

129

regional economic power is southern Africa, and United States–based investments there have grown from $286 million in 1960 . . . to $1.7 billion in 1977.

United States–based companies have claimed that their presence in southern Africa contributes to stability and meaningful social change. However, during the decades of expanding United States investments, political repression of the African majority has increased. The gap between white wealth and black poverty has widened. United States companies have generally followed the racist laws and customs in southern Africa. In addition, they have supplied strategic equipment, technology, and financial resources which strengthen the white minorities in southern Africa.

For example, key areas of United States private investments in South Africa include:

(a) Banks: United States–based banks have loaned more than two billion dollars to South Africa. Loans are made directly to the South African government and its agencies. These loans act as an economic vote of confidence in the white minority government and aid in increasing its military strength. Manufacturers Hanover Trust, Bank of America, Chase Manhattan, First National City Bank of Chicago, Continental Bank of Illinois, Citibank, and Morgan Guaranty Trust are the major American banks which have made loans to South Africa.

(b) Oil: The oil industry is an especially strategic sector in South Africa, which has no reserves of its own and is dependent on foreign supplies. For example, Mobil and Caltex are the major oil suppliers to the South African regime and sell oil to Rhodesia through South Africa.

(c) Technology: IBM supplies 50 per cent of South Africa's computer needs, and other American computer firms operate in the country as well.

In addition, United States–based companies are also involved in other strategic sectors of the South African economy such as transportation, mining, and communications. United States firms also play varying roles in the economies of Namibia and Rhodesia. A high percentage of United States investments in Namibia is represented by the Tsumeb Corporation, which is jointly owned by Newmont Mining Corporation, AMAX (both United States–based companies), and others. The Tsumeb Corporation alone accounts for more than 80 per cent of Namibia's production in base metals, almost all of which is exported.

The major United States investments in Rhodesia are represented by Union Carbide and other mining companies. In order to avoid defiance of United Nations sanctions, subsidiaries of United States companies were placed under local control of the white regime, but the basic United States corporate interest remains.

UNITED STATES GOVERNMENT POLICY

In the past several years, southern Africa has become an important foreign policy issue for the United States government. Before 1960, Africa as a whole was given very little attention by the United States government because of the widespread domination of Africa by European colonial powers. As African nationalist movements for independence arose following World War II, Africa did receive more consideration. However, the United States tended to support colonial policies. The State Department did not establish an Africa Bureau until the early 1960s.

With regard to southern Africa in particular, the United States consistently expressed verbal support for racial justice but took no concrete steps to support majority rule. In fact, United States duplicity on southern Africa was clearly spelled out in a secret study, *National Security Study Memorandum 39* (NSSM39), prepared for the National Security Council and signed by Henry Kissinger in 1969. Its overriding assumption was that white minority regimes would remain firmly in power in southern Africa and could not be successfully challenged by the African majorities. Therefore, the study reasoned, whatever changes might occur to improve the situation of blacks could only take place with white consent and under white control. Of the policy options contained in the memorandum, the one selected for implementation involved not only a toning down of verbal criticism of the white regimes, but also increased diplomatic, military, technological, and economic support.

However, the premise that white rule could not be successfully challenged in southern Africa was shattered when, in 1974, the pressure of the liberation movements in Mozambique and Angola precipitated a coup d'état in Portugal. The victories of Frelimo in Mozambique and MPLA in Angola broke the seemingly stable block of white minority regimes in southern Africa. New elements were therefore introduced which could not be ignored in any formulation of policy regarding southern Africa.

Today, the question for the United States is no longer whether majority rule is possible. The question is what is the best way to achieve it. The United States has publicly expressed its commitment to peaceful change in southern Africa. In the meantime, the level of rhetorical commitment to majority rule and to social change has been increased by the United States. But the situation demands concrete actions. The United States must not continue rhetorically to endorse majority rule, while economically, politically, diplomatically, and militarily supporting white minority rule.

AFFIRMATIONS

(1) LIBERATION: In its Resolution on the Churches' Policy Toward Southern Africa, adopted by the General Assembly on December 6, 1972, the National Council of the Churches of Christ in the U.S.A. (NCCC) affirmed a concern for liberation in the following statement:

As members of the National Council of the Churches of Christ in the U.S.A., we seek continuously to be true to Christ's mission "to proclaim release to the captives and to set at liberty those who are oppressed." We understand Christ as the one who liberates people, freeing them from dehumanizing cultures and systems, freeing them from the bondage of racial and religious discrimination, and freeing them from inhumanities which result from one group or nation of people exploiting another.

We again affirm support for the liberation of the people of southern Africa in their struggle to regain control of their land, their freedom, and their dignity—birthrights of every human creature of God.

In Namibia, South Africa, and Zimbabwe, the call for liberation is urgent.

(2) MAJORITY RULE: In a resolution adopted by the Governing Board on October 9, 1976, the NCCC reaffirmed its commitment to majority rule in southern Africa. In the same spirit, the Council condemned the complicity of the United States military and business interests with the racist minorities which rule in South Africa,

Zimbabwe, and Namibia. The Council commended those Christians and other persons who, by word and deed, have committed themselves to the struggle to bring about majority rule.

(3) SELF-DETERMINATION: The NCCC, in its Resolution on the Churches' Policy Toward Southern Africa, adopted by the General Assembly on December 6, 1972, stated:

In concert with Christ's mission in the world and the church's mission to the disinherited of this world, we express our commitment to, and support for, the oppressed black peoples of southern Africa. We affirm the courageous acts of the black majorities in southern Africa as they seek to remove the yokes of oppression to achieve human dignity and self-determination.

The right of peoples and nations to self-determination is a prerequisite to the full enjoyment of all fundamental human rights as defined in the "Universal Declaration of Human Rights." We affirm that the concept of self-determination includes the rights of people to choose their own economic, social, and political systems without external economic, political, or military coercion. We affirm this right of self-determination for the people of southern Africa.

Included in the right to self-determination is the right not to have one's land partitioned by outside forces. This is particularly important to the peoples of southern Africa. On October 9, 1976, the NCCC Governing Board adopted the Resolution on the Transkei, which condemned the projected policy of establishing "homelands" or bantustans as a device by the South African government to divide in order to control. The Resolution stated that this process would deprive black South Africans simultaneously of much of their lands, and their South African citizenship and attendant rights to which they are entitled. The Resolution followed the spirit of the United Nations' action which had called upon "all Governments and organizations not to deal with any institutions or authorities of the bantustans or to accord any form of recognition to them."

We renew our condemnation of any effort aiming at the "balkanization" of the southern Africa nations. Along with the majority of the nations of the world, the Council condemns the South African government's hypocritical insistence on proclaiming independence for the bantustans.

(4) RACIAL JUSTICE: Among the general principles stated in the National Council of Churches' human rights policy adopted by the General Assembly on December 6, 1963, was the following:

All rich gifts which God imparts to [people] should be available without discrimination as to creed, race, color, sex, birth, nationality, economic or social status. So the National Council of Churches has denounced and reaffirms its denunciation of patterns of segregation as contrary to the will of God for [human unity].

We affirm that all persons of every color are of equal worth in the sight of God and that human institutions, political or otherwise, which deny human worth on the basis of race are sinful.

We reaffirm our denunciation of all systems which discriminate against persons on the basis of race.

(5) HUMAN RIGHTS:

Christians believe that each [person] is made in the image of God, that every [person] is of intrinsic worth before God, and that every individual has a right to the fullest possible opportunities for the development of life abundant and eternal. Denials of rights and freedoms that inhere in a [person's] worth before God are not simply a crime against humanity; they are a sin against God.

The National Council of Churches stated this conviction in its human rights policy statement (December 6, 1963). While affirming the United Nations Universal Declaration of Human Rights, the policy statement pointed out that a specific program of action for achieving the objectives of the Declaration is still lacking. The Council expressed this concern again as it relates to southern Africa in its Resolution on Southern Africa, adopted by the Governing Board in October 1976, which stated that the Council was particularly concerned about the flagrant violations of human rights to which the African majority in South Africa, Namibia, and Zimbabwe continues to be subjected.

In the context of this deep concern for the systematic denial of human rights in southern Africa and in the context of the NCCC's affirmation of the Universal Declaration of Human Rights, we affirm that the peoples of southern Africa have the right to the full range of political, economic, social, and cultural rights, all of which are interrelated and mutually reinforcing.

DECLARATIONS

The Governing Board of the National Council of the Churches of Christ in the U.S.A., recognizing the grave injustices in southern Africa, and guided by its commitment to Christian principles and its own affirmations of human rights, declares its support for the following actions:

1. NAMIBIA

(a) Support programs of the churches, of the South West Africa People's Organization (SWAPO), and other Namibian organizations which are struggling for the liberation of Namibia.

(b) Support United Nations Security Council Resolution 385, which calls for the withdrawal of South Africa and free elections under United Nations supervision and control based upon the principle of one-person-one-vote.

(c) Support efforts to discourage investments by multinational corporations in Namibia until independence is attained.

(d) Support programs of assistance for refugees, political detainees, and others who suffer because of the oppressive situation in Namibia.

(e) Monitor United States government policies relating to Namibia and disseminate information for public education.

2. SOUTH AFRICA

(a) Support efforts to end all economic collaboration between South Africa and the United States government and its private institutions involved in banking, commerce, and industry, until black majority rule is a reality.

(b) Support efforts to end all military collaboration between the United States and South Africa.

(c) Support persons, churches, and other organizations in South Africa which are directly involved in the struggle for liberation and racial justice.

(d) Support programs of assistance for refugees, political prisoners, and others who suffer because of the denial of human rights.

(e) Monitor United States government policies relating to South Africa and disseminate information for public education.

(f) Undertake to withdraw all funds and close all accounts in financial institutions which have investments in South Africa or make loans to the South African government or businesses, and urge constituent membership to adopt this policy.

3. ZIMBABWE

(a) Support an immediate transfer of power to the African majority.

(b) Support and strengthen the continuation of economic sanctions against the government of Rhodesia.

(c) Support the churches and those political organizations which are struggling for a free Zimbabwe.

(d) Support programs of assistance for refugees, political detainees, and others who suffer because of the repressive situation in Zimbabwe.

(e) Monitor United States government policies relating to Zimbabwe and disseminate information for public education.

4. UNITED NATIONS DECADE FOR ACTION TO COMBAT RACISM

In addition, the Governing Board urges the United States government as further evidence of its commitment to human rights and the elimination of racism to give strong support to the United Nations Decade for Action to Combat Racism and Racial Discrimination.

Investment in South Africa

A Statement by
Mangosuthu Gatsha Buthelezi

*Chief Buthelezi is the chief minister of KwaZulu (a non-indepen-
dent black homeland), the president of the black political and cultural organization Inkatha, and the chairman of the South African Black Alliance. The
following is excerpted from his address to a group of visiting U.S. investors at
a seminar in Durban in September 1983.*

EACH INDUSTRIAL NATION to some extent is an island unto itself, but in broader
perspective, in the same way that one western or American national economy is
intimately related to the other western economies, generally speaking it will be linked
by fate to the Third World, and the South African connection in this link is an
important one. I believe that it is globally important for the South African economy to
be liberalized to the extent that a true free enterprise system evolves in this country.
Foreign investment could play an important role in liberating the economy from
ideological controls and should be encouraged. I do not want to go further afield in
discussing investment decisions at this level because I am not an international financier
or an economist, and wish only to make some observations from the perspective of the
peasant background from which I come. As a boy I herded goats and cattle in the fields
and grew up amongst peasants in a rural area. Many of my intimate associates have
remained peasants and workers. . . .

Having come from a peasant background and having been in politics for something
like thirty years, I am in a position to talk about black South Africa with, I hope, some
authority. I want to emphasize that the perspectives you will hear from me today are not
those of an individual expressing personal opinions. I have managed to build up
Inkatha as a mass movement with well above 750,000 card-carrying members, and I
have done this over a short period of eight years. Inkatha was born in 1975 and rose
like a colossus through the 1976-78 period of black civic protest. It was born during
South African events in which there was a dramatic heightening of black political
consciousness, and Inkatha is growing as vigorously in 1983 as it did in its earlier
years. The graph of membership is ascending at the same rate, and as yet there are no
signs of its leveling off. Inkatha is black South Africa in political ascendance.

I make the point about Inkatha as a South African political phenomenon of this
country as a prelude to saying that in my leadership I capture the idiom of the people,
and in the democratic mechanisms and procedures which so strongly characterize
Inkatha I am made intimately aware of black public opinion. Inkatha is as represen-

Reprinted by permission of the South Africa Foundation from *South Africa International*, vol. 14,
no. 4 (April 1984).

tative of urban black South Africa as it is of rural South Africa. It is a cross-section of black South African society unparalleled in the history of this country. No political leader could have built up such a vast political force if he did not embody in his person the views and aspirations of the ordinary people of the country. Whenever I speak, I speak against the background of knowing that I have to return to my people and tell them what I have said. I am their voice, and I do not follow double agendas. I am not one thing in Durban and another thing in New York. An analysis of what I have said over the years will show a very high degree of consistency. This is so because I articulate the views of a very determined people with very specific objectives. Whatever is said about investment in overseas lobbies should be tested against what the people in South Africa themselves say.

In any society there is consensus in majority opinion on crucial matters, and there are also minority groups deviating from a general view. This is as true on the question of investment as it is for any other question. There are black South Africans, and their voice is not insignificant, who have grown disillusioned with the West; they have grown disillusioned with capitalism and the free enterprise system, and they argue for a socialist future. Those who hold this minority view can at times be tragically careless about industrial and worker well-being as they devise tactics and strategies that are aimed at bringing about radical political change in the shortest possible space of time.

When we go beyond talking about black South Africa we must realize that in white South Africa there is also a minority group that is careless about the future of this country as it seeks to establish permanent white political supremacy in the shortest possible space of time. We have therefore two minority groups, one black seeking radical change towards a socialist future in the shortest possible time, and one white seeking the circumstances of perpetuated white racist domination in the shortest possible time. It is these two groups who catch the investor in their cross-fire. The disinvestment debate and the disinvestment lobbyists fail to perceive this position, and I have found that extremely sophisticated western investors become confused in the rhetoric that flies back and forth.

Both minority groups claim universal support for their contentions. Disinvestment lobbyists will tell you in the United States that black South Africa has reached the end of its tether and that the black population very definitely supports the campaign in the West directed at discouraging investment and isolating South Africa economically. The white minority seeking finally to entrench their racial superiority will tell you that the vast majority of South Africans, including blacks, support apartheid and that the ongoing system in this country is one in which South Africans generally see their greatest benefits.

I who root my life and my politics in the masses of the ordinary people do not have to involve myself in rhetoric, and in a sense I stand aside from this scene of rhetorical exchanges and can afford to look at it objectively. I, like black South Africa as a whole, am aware that the black people in South Africa support neither the system of apartheid nor the political forces that want to produce radical changes overnight to thrust us into a utopian socialist future tomorrow.

Poverty is a hard taskmaster. It teaches us what reality is and makes us intimately aware of the consequences of political blundering. Black South Africa now has two generations of experience behind it in a struggle for liberation, and in that experience it has again and again been acquainted with false political prophets advocating unrealistic strategies that achieve nothing but the increased suffering of the people. It can be simply and safely said that an assessment of the South African situation will be inaccurate if it revolves around assessments of the merits of the rhetoric that emanates from white right-wing South Africa and black left-wing South Africa. What actually happens in this country and what will happen in the future will not be orchestrated by rhetorical leadership. History is not herded before rhetorical spokesmen. It is the consequence, rather, of that intricate interrelationship between myriads of individual and group vested interests. . . .

Something like more than half of South Africa's African population is 15 years of age or younger, and one of the driving motives in adult Africans is to secure a better future for their children. Against the history of two generations of African suffering in apartheid South Africa, there is an adult acceptance that there are no quick and easy solutions and there are no utopias; there is an acceptance that there is a struggle for liberation that has been a long and hard one and could well remain so for some time to come.

In 1981 I established the Buthelezi Commission to examine the whole question of KwaZulu's location in Natal and South Africa and to seek a consensus view on how we should tackle the question of bringing about change and in what direction that change should move. Commissioners were drawn from every walk of life and from all race groups. The business community was represented on the Commission by members of the Institute of Bankers in South Africa, the Natal Chamber of Industries, the Durban Chamber of Commerce, the South African Institute of Civil Engineers, the KwaZulu Development Corporation, Anglo-American Corporation, the Associated Chamber of Commerce, the Natal Sugar Industry, the South African Federated Chamber of Industries, Inyanda Chamber of Commerce, and the National African Federated Chamber of Commerce.

In the broad range of their considerations, the commissioners called for scientific surveys of black attitudes and black aspirations. In one of the questionnaires used in the scientific surveys conducted, this question was posed: "If the government were to ask people like you about improving the lives of black South Africans today, which of the following should it do?" . . . Respondents were allowed to pick more than one of the suggested improvements. [The statements in order of preference are] as follows:

1. *equalize education:* 72 per cent
2. *give higher wages to blacks:* 69 per cent
3. *remove influx control:* 44 per cent
4. *extend the franchise to black South Africans:* 33 per cent
5. *curb price rises:* 30 per cent
6. *release imprisoned leaders:* 29 per cent
7. *make home ownership possible:* 16 per cent
8. *divide white farms for black South Africans to buy:* 8 per cent
9. *permit blacks to purchase homes in white suburbs:* 7 per cent
10. *open social facilities:* 3 per cent

This then is the profile of black South Africans I am talking to you about. It is a profile of a realistic people knowing what their priorities are. When the sample was broken down into metropolitan and rural groups, the pattern remained generally the same with only relatively minor differences, which can be related to life circumstances.

Black South Africans generally perceive the future as one in which benefits will be derived from relying on themselves. The high ranking given to improved educational needs can be traced to this fact. Black South Africans are not ideological idealists out of touch with reality, and it is for this reason that I have repeatedly encouraged white South Africa in general, and industrialists in particular, to build upon the human material that is available for development in black South Africa. There is in this country a vast task force committed to progress and development, which matches the economic opportunity provided by the mineral wealth of the country and its existing industrial base.

In the pursuit of personal, social, and economic objectives, black South Africans have ranked job opportunities high in their list of priorities. They have thus always supported job-creating investments in this country, and it is simply not true that the vast majority of blacks support the disinvestment lobby. We recognize that there can be no real political progress in this country unless the veritable sea of destitution around us is eliminated. If we are to have a negotiated future, we recognize that on our side the strength of our negotiating position is directly related to our necessity to whites, and we recognize that we are very much more necessary in factories than in impoverished unemployed communities. The drive to make South Africa a better place for ourselves and for our children enhances for us the value of working.

But whenever I have talked about black South Africa, I have talked about it in the context of black South Africa's perceived options. I have repeatedly warned that there is already a minority of blacks who abandon hope in the future if it is to remain rooted in white vested interests. They see white South Africa as incapable of abandoning its privileged position and incapable of sharing its economic, social, and political advantages voluntarily. They see white racism as unchanging if it is left to its own devices, and they see the need to force whites to change through revolutionary activity. They see capitalism and the free enterprise system as bastions of white strength, and they see the need to destroy these systems and to replace them with a people's republic based on socialist ideals. I have repeatedly warned both investors and white South Africa that the good will and the commitment towards orderly progress in this country in black South Africa is a national asset that must not be wasted and mismanaged politically. . . .

Notes

CHAPTER ONE

1. P. W. Botha, address at opening of parliament, Cape Town, September 15, 1984.

2. Desmond Tutu, "Reform, South Africa Style," *Washington Post*, March 18, 1984, p. C7.

3. "Redecorating Apartheid," *New York Times*, October 17, 1983, p. A20.

4. "The Word From South Africa," *Washington Post*, November 6, 1983, p. D6.

5. "A Yes for Botha," *The Economist*, October 22, 1983, p. 15.

6. Raymond D. Gastil, ed., *Freedom in the World: Political Rights and Civil Liberties, 1983-1984* (Westport, Conn.: Greenwood Press, 1982), p. 426.

7. Study Commission on U.S. Policy Toward Southern Africa, *South Africa: Time Running Out* (Berkeley: University of California Press, 1981), p. 310.

8. Richard Nixon, *The Real War* (New York: Warner Books, 1980), p. 30.

9. Quoted ibid., p. 23.

10. Study Commission on U.S. Policy, *South Africa: Time Running Out*, p. 133ff.

11. John H. Chettle, "Economic Relations Between South Africa and Black Africa," *SAIS Review*, vol. 4, no. 2 (Summer-Fall 1984), p. 131.

12. Statistics cited in Pat Poovalingham, "The Impact of Cultural and Economic Disengagement From South Africa on Intercommunity Relations," in Nic J. Rhoodie, ed., *Conflict Resolution in South Africa* (Pretoria: Institute of Plural Societies, University of Pretoria, 1980), p. 219.

13. Study Commission on U.S. Policy, *South Africa: Time Running Out*, pp. 128-29.

14. American Chamber of Commerce in South Africa, *U.S. Business Involvement in South Africa*, January 1984, p. 17.

15. See John Western, "Social Engineering Through Spatial Manipulation: Apartheid in South African Cities," in Colin Clarke et al., eds., *Geography and Ethnic Pluralism* (London: George Allen and Unwin, 1984), esp. pp. 117-25.

16. Steve Manyane, "Forced Removals," *South Africa Foundation News*, October 1984, p. 2.

17. Neil Ulman, "South African Black Taps Emerging Market," *Wall Street Journal*, June 18, 1984, p. 26.

18. Quoted in Neil Ulman, "South Africa's Blacks Make Some Advances But Still Lack Power," *Wall Street Journal*, June 19, 1984, p. 20. See also Gavin Relly, "Personal Mobility and the South African Economy: Lifting Curbs on Opportunity," *South Africa International*, January 1984, pp. 476-82.

19. Samuel P. Huntington, "Will More Countries Become Democratic?," *Political Science Quarterly*, vol. 99, no. 2 (Summer 1984), pp. 216-17.

20. See John H. Chettle, "The Law and Policy of Divestment of South African Stock," *Law and Policy in International Business*, vol. 15, no. 2 (1983), pp. 445-528.

21. See Chester A. Crocker, "South Africa: Strategy for Change," *Foreign Affairs*, Winter 1980/81.

22. "Reagan Policy Has 'Opened Doors'—Crocker," *Africa News*, Nov. 14, 1983.

23. Ibid.

24. U.S. Department of State, Bureau of Public Affairs, "Southern Africa: America's Responsibility for Peace and Change," *Current Policy* no. 407 (June 23, 1983).

25. U.S. Department of State, Bureau of Public Affairs, "The U.S. and Africa in the 1980s," *Current Policy* no. 549 (February 15, 1984), p. 4.

26. Lawrence Litvak, Robert DeGrasse, and Kathleen McTigue, *South Africa: Foreign Investment and Apartheid* (Washington: Institute for Policy Studies, 1978), p. 43.

27. Philip L. Christenson, "United States–South African Economic Relations: Major Issues in the United States," in Alfred O. Hero, Jr., and John Barratt, eds., *The American People and South Africa* (Lexington, Mass.: Lexington Books, 1981), pp. 52-53.

28. Ibid., p. 53.

29. Desaix Myers III, "U.S. Domestic Controversy over American Business in South Africa," in ibid., p. 68.

30. James Cason and Michael Fleshman, "Dollar$ for Apartheid," *Multinational Monitor*, November 1983, p. 19.

31. Frank Wisner, testimony, *Internal Political Situation in South Africa* (U.S. Congress, House, Foreign Affairs Committee, Subcommittee on Africa, Sept. 14, 1983), pp. 113-14.

32. Vella Pillay, "Transnationals in South Africa," *Journal of African Marxists*, no. 3 (January 1983), p. 99.

33. Paraphrased in Ernest W. Lefever, *Revolution, Terrorism, and U.S. Policy* (Washington: Ethics and Public Policy Center, 1983).

34. Quoted in Margaret A. Novicki, "Interview with the Reverend Allan Boesak," *Africa Report*, July-August 1983, p. 8.

35. See, *inter alia*, Kofi Appiah-Kubi and Sergio Torres, eds., *African Theology En Route* (Maryknoll, N.Y.: Orbis Books, 1979), esp. Desmond Tutu, "The Theology of Liberation in Africa," pp. 162-68, and Allan Boesak, "Liberation Theology in South Africa," pp. 169-75; Gustavo Gutiérrez, *A Theology of Liberation* (Maryknoll, N.Y.: Orbis Books, 1973); Marjorie Hope and James Young, *The South African Churches in a Revolutionary Situation* (Maryknoll, N.Y.: Orbis Books, 1981); Edward R. Norman, *Christianity and the World Order* (New York: Oxford University Press, 1979); Haddon Willmer et al., *Christian Faith and Political Hopes: A Reply to E. R. Norman* (London: Epworth Press, 1979); and Quentin L. Quade, ed., *The Pope and Revolution: John Paul II Confronts Liberation Theology* (Washington: Ethics and Public Policy Center, 1982).

36. See Allan Boesak, *Walking on Thorns: The Call to Christian Disobedience* (Geneva: World Council of Churches, 1984), esp. pp. 19-25.

CHAPTER TWO

1. See Joseph A. Harriss, "Karl Marx or Jesus Christ?," *Reader's Digest*, August 1982; Paul Abrecht, "Ecumenical Illiteracy in the 'Reader's Digest,'" *The Christian Century*, November 24, 1982; James M. Wall, "Ecumenical Agencies Under Attack," *The Christian Century*, September 1-8, 1982; CBS News, "The Gospel According to Whom?," *60 Minutes*, January 23, 1983; and special editions of *The United Methodist Reporter*, April 8 and April 16, 1983.

2. See Ernest W. Lefever, *Amsterdam to Nairobi: The World Council of Churches and the Third World* (Washington: Ethics and Public Policy Center, 1979), pp. 34-35 and appendix H, pp. 102-4.

3. Quoted in Leon Howell, "South Africa and the Attack on the Churches," *Washington Notes on Africa*, Autumn 1983, p. 1.

4. *Findings and Decisions, First Assembly of the World Council of Churches* (Geneva: World Council of Churches, 1948).

5. W. A. Visser 't Hooft, ed., *The Evanston Report* (New York: Harper and Brothers, 1955).

6. W. A. Visser 't Hooft, ed., *The New Delhi Report* (New York: Association Press, 1962).

7. Norman Goodall, ed., *The Uppsala Report* (Geneva: World Council of Churches, 1968), p. 66.

8. *Uppsala to Nairobi* (New York: Friendship Press, 1975).

9. Baldwin Sjollema, *Isolating Apartheid* (Geneva: World Council of Churches, 1982), appendix F, pp. 128-36.

10. Ibid., p. 129.

11. Resolution adopted September 29, 1978. Reprinted in George Austin, *World Council of Churches Programme to Combat Racism*, Conflict Studies no. 105 (London: Institute for the Study of Conflict, March 1979), pp. 19, 20.

12. Sjollema, *Isolating Apartheid*, pp. 128-36.

13. Two volumes of hearings and a committee report on "The Role of the Soviet Union, Cuba, and East Germany in Fomenting Terrorism in Southern Africa" were published by the Subcommittee on Security and Terrorism of the U.S. Senate Committee on the Judiciary (1982). Testimony there explains the extent of Communist involvement in the ANC, PAC, and SWAPO. For a somewhat different view, see Thomas G. Karis, "Black Politics in South Africa," *Foreign Affairs*, Winter 1983/84, pp. 378-406.

14. "Church Council Aids Apartheid Fight," *Washington Times*, September 27, 1984, p. 5A.

15. Lefever, *Amsterdam to Nairobi*, pp. 31-37, 91-101.

16. Sjollema, *Isolating Apartheid*, p. 129.

17. *The World Council of Churches and Bank Loans to Apartheid* (Geneva: WCC, 1977), p. 6.

18. *Time to Withdraw: Investments in Southern Africa* (Geneva: World Council of Churches Program to Combat Racism, 1973), p. 1.

19. Ibid., p. 16.

20. Ibid.

21. Sjollema, *Isolating Apartheid*, p. 59.

22. Ibid., pp. 59-60.

23. Ibid.

24. Ibid., p. 106.

25. Ibid., p. 105.

26. Ibid., p. 107.

27. Dorothee Sölle, "Life in Its Fullness," Document TH3-1, World Council of Churches Sixth Assembly, 24 July–10 August 1983, p. 5.

28. Ulrich Duchrow, "Struggling for Justice and Human Dignity," Document GR6-1, World Council of Churches Sixth Assembly, 24 July–10 August 1983, p. 3.

29. Ibid.

30. "Southern Africa," Document PR 2-11 (second part), World Council of Churches Sixth Assembly, 24 July–10 August 1983, p. 4. Published in David Gill, ed., *Gathered for Life* (Grand Rapids, Mich.: Eerdmans, 1984), pp. 156-57.

31. Quoted in Sjollema, *Isolating Apartheid*, p. 6.

32. Quoted ibid., p. 107.

33. Ibid., p. 14.

34. Marjorie Hope and James Young, *The South African Churches in a Revolutionary Situation* (Maryknoll, N.Y.: Orbis Books, 1981), p. 3.

35. Howell, "South Africa and the Attack on the Churches," p. 1.

36. Prexy Nesbitt, "African Liberation Movements Versus 'Rawhide and Rainbow': A Note on the Reagan Administration's Policies in Southern Africa," *PCR Information: The Churches' Involvement in Southern Africa* (1982/No. 14), p. 21. This article referred to President Reagan as "a failed Hollywood actor."

CHAPTER THREE

1. James Young, "South African Churches: Agents of Change," *The Christian Century,* November 24, 1982, p. 1201.

2. *South Africa 1983: Official Yearbook of the Republic of South Africa* (Johannesburg: Chris van Rensburg Publications, 1983), "Religion," pp. 765-84. There is a misprint on p. 783: according to table 4, there are 11.5 million black Methodists; the correct number is 1.5 million.

3. Quoted in Marjorie Hope and James Young, *The South African Churches in a Revolutionary Situation* (Maryknoll, N.Y.: Orbis Books, 1981), back cover.

4. *South Africa 1979: Official Yearbook of the Republic of South Africa* (Johannesburg: Chris van Rensburg Publications, 1979), pp. 790-91.

5. Interview with Margaret A. Novicki, *Africa Report,* July-August 1983, p. 7.

6. Alan Paton, Foreword, in John W. de Gruchy, *The Church Struggle in South Africa* (Grand Rapids, Mich.: Eerdmans, 1979), p. viii.

7. Charles Villa-Vicencio, "The Church: Discordant and Divided," *Africa Report,* July-August 1983, p. 13.

8. Ibid., p. 15.

9. See John W. de Gruchy and Charles Villa-Vicencio, eds., *Apartheid Is a Heresy* (Grand Rapids, Mich.: Eerdmans, 1983), appendix, pp. 144-84.

10. G.S.J. Moller and L. Moolman, "The Dutch Reformed Church and Separate Development," *Africa Report,* July-August 1983, p. 39. The authors note: "There are no statistics available of how many members of the NGK are also full members of the Nationalist party. All the existing political parties count members of the NGK among their supporters. . . . The fact is that the NGK has no official ties with any of the political parties" (p. 40).

11. Quoted in David Thomas, "Church-State Relations in South Africa: Uncomfortable Bedfellows," *South Africa International,* July 1982, p. 51.

12. De Gruchy, *Church Struggle in South Africa,* p. 219.

13. Allister Sparks, "S. African Church Faces Breakup," *Washington Post,* October 27, 1982.

14. Nederduitsch Hervormde Kerk, "Statement on the WARC Decision," September 17, 1982, in de Gruchy and Villa-Vicencio, *Apartheid Is a Heresy,* p. 174.

15. Ibid.

16. Nederduitse Gereformeerde Kerk, "Resolution on the WARC Decision," October 27, 1982, in de Gruchy and Villa-Vicencio, *Apartheid Is a Heresy,* p. 184.

17. Interview with Novicki, p. 12.

18. Nederduitse Gereformeerde Sendingkerk, "A Statement on Apartheid and a Confession of Faith," 1982, in de Gruchy and Villa-Vicencio, *Apartheid Is a Heresy,* p. 182. (Scripture translation not indicated.)

19. Thomas, "Church-State Relations in South Africa," p. 49.

20. Calvin W. Cook, "What the Bible Teaches About Church and State," in John de Gruchy and W. B. de Villiers, eds., *The Message in Perspective* (Pretoria: South African Council of Churches, 1968), p. 52.

21. David Thomas, *Councils in the Ecumenical Movement in South Africa, 1904-1975* (Johannesburg: South African Council of Churches, 1979), pp. 115-16.

22. An excellent discussion of the "Message" and the controversy it set off is in de

Gruchy, *The Church Struggle in South Africa,* pp. 115-27. The full text of the "Message" is found in de Gruchy and Villa-Vicencio, *Apartheid Is a Heresy,* pp. 154-59.

23. De Gruchy and Villa-Vicencio, *Apartheid Is a Heresy,* p. 155.

24. Ibid, p. 159.

25. Peter Walshe, "Church Versus State in South Africa," *Journal of Church and State,* Autumn 1977, p. 462.

26. David Thomas, ed., *Investment in South Africa,* Report Submitted by the Division of Justice and Reconciliation to the National Conference of the South African Council of Churches, Hammanskraal, July 26-28, 1977 (Johannesburg: South African Council of Churches, 1977), p. 31.

27. Ibid.

28. Ibid., p. 19.

29. "Jail Threat Has Silenced Many," *Natal Witness,* July 21, 1978.

30. "Tutu Urges Cash Pressure on South Africa," *Rand Daily Mail,* July 21, 1978.

31. "Bishop Tutu Faces Stormy Meeting," *The Citizen* (Johannesburg), November 24, 1978.

32. *Ecunews Bulletin,* September 14, 1979, pp. 10-11.

33. Desmond Tutu, *Crying in the Wilderness: The Struggle for Justice in South Africa* (Grand Rapids, Mich.: Eerdmans, 1982), p. 53.

34. Desmond Tutu, "We Who Are Oppressed Will Be Free," *Washington Post,* October 17, 1984, p. A15 (excerpts from September 23, 1981, article).

35. Sharon Mielke, "S. African Investment Guidelines Denounced," *United Methodist Reporter,* August 26, 1983, p. 4.

36. Ibid.

37. Ibid.

38. Tutu, *Crying in the Wilderness,* pp. 97-100.

39. Ibid., p. 112.

40. Esther B. Fein, "South African Foe of Apartheid Wins the 1984 Nobel Peace Prize; Bells Peal on 9th Avenue," *New York Times,* October 17, 1984, p. A15.

41. Jim Hoagland, "S. African Bishop Wins Nobel," *Washington Post,* October 17, 1984, p. A25.

42. Quoted in Allister Sparks, "S. Africa's Laureate," *Washington Post,* October 19, 1984, p. A32.

43. John F. Burns, "Black Bishop and South Africa," *New York Times,* May 4, 1980.

44. Johannesburg *Star,* August 8, 1980.

45. Thomas, "Church-State Relations in South Africa," p. 60.

46. "Report of Provincial Commission on Foreign Investments in Southern Africa," mimeographed (submitted to the Provincial Standing Commission, November 1977).

47. Methodist Church of Southern Africa, *Minutes of the Conference,* 1981, p. 274.

48. Felician A. Foy, ed., *The 1974 Catholic Almanac* (Huntington, Ind.: Our Sunday Visitor, 1974). See also *South Africa 1979,* pp. 785-86.

49. See Denis E. Hurley, "South Africa: The Catholic Church and Apartheid," *Africa Report,* July-August 1983, pp. 17-19.

50. Stuart C. Bate and Roddy Nunes, "A Call to Workers and Employers," in *The Bishops Speak: Volume II, Pastoral Letters and Statements 1967-1980* (Pretoria: Southern African Catholic Bishops' Conference, 1980), p. 122.

51. Cited by Georgetown University treasurer George R. Houston in interview with Paul Weinstein, Jr., "Houston Evaluates S. Africa Policy," *The Georgetown Voice,* October 20, 1981, p. 4. Cf. Beth Partin, "Anti-Apartheid at GU," *The Georgetown*

Voice, April 3, 1984, pp. 6-8, where Houston reiterates this view.

52. Remarks cited in "Big Business May Turn Against Apartheid," *National Catholic Register*, March 21, 1982, p. 2. (Abridged version of Stephanie Overman, "Industry May Turn Against Apartheid, Archbishop Hurley Says," National Catholic News Service, March 9, 1982, pp. 3-4.)

53. Walshe, "Church Versus State in South Africa," p. 461.

54. Christian Institute of Southern Africa, "Investment in South Africa," in *The World Council of Churches and Bank Loans to Apartheid* (Geneva: World Council of Churches, 1977), p. 65.

55. Ibid.

56. Ibid., p. 66.

57. Letter from Trevor M. Swart to the author, May 27, 1983.

58. Letter from M. L. Badenhorst to the author, March 3, 1983.

59. Ibid.

60. Statement of the Church of England in South Africa, December 12, 1979, p. 1.

61. Letter from Herbert Hammond to the author, April 7, 1983.

62. Letter from J. P. Erasmus to the author, March 18, 1983.

63. Ibid.

64. Quoted in letter from P. B. Hoyer, moderator, Maranatha Pentecostal Church, to the author, February 21, 1983.

65. Letter from E. J. Duschinsky to the author, February 28, 1983. Rabbi Duschinsky notes, however: "I do not like to imply that the above is representing a general, or even majority, view of my colleagues in the Jewish Rabbinate."

66. Letter from Herbert Hammond.

67. The conclusions of this chapter were supported in interviews with seventeen South African church leaders conducted by Ernest W. Lefever, August 2-17, 1979. Only one of the seventeen, Bishop Desmond Tutu, argued in favor of disinvestment. The others favored continued investment from abroad. They were: Dr. D. P. M. Beukes, NGK; Dr. Allan Boesak, NG Sendingkerk (now president of World Alliance of Reformed Churches); Dr. Dawie Botha, NG Sendingkerk; Pastor C. Brandt, Evangelical Lutheran Church in Southern Africa; the Rev. Abel Hendricks, ex-president of the Methodist Church of Southern Africa; Dr. W. A. Landman, NGK; Dr. Ben Marais, NGK; the Reverend E. M. Mataboge, NGK in Africa; Cardinal Owen McCann, Roman Catholic archbishop of Cape Town; Bishop Michael Nuttall, Anglican; Dr. F. E. O'Brien, NGK; Dr. A. B. Pont, professor of church history, University of Pretoria; the Rev. Fred Shaw, Christian League of Southern Africa; Bishop Swarts, Anglican; the Rev. J. A. Tshabalala, Methodist; and Dr. J. van Rooyen, NGK.

CHAPTER FOUR

1. J. Brian Sheehan, ed., "A Symposium on Current Issues Facing American Corporations in South Africa," September 28, 1981 (transcript available from General Motors, Ford Motor Co., and Interfaith Center on Corporate Responsibility), p. 11.

2. Charles Austin, "Business-Church Accord on South Africa Is Elusive," *New York Times*, September 30, 1981, p. B4.

3. Ibid.

4. Ibid.

5. Interfaith Center on Corporate Responsibility, "Excerpts from Speeches at a 'Symposium on Current Issues Facing American Corporations in South Africa,'" *ICCR Brief*, February 1982, p. 4.

6. Ibid., p. 2.

7. Austin, "Business-Church Accord."

8. Ibid.

9. Ibid.

10. Charles Austin, "Diverging Views on Disinvestment," *The Christian Century,* October 28, 1981, pp. 1084-85.

11. Robert J. Flaherty, "Revolution, Sayeth the Churchman—One Soul at a Time, Says a Businessman," *Forbes,* February 6, 1978, p. 31.

12. Ibid., p. 33.

13. Interfaith Center on Corporate Responsibility Annual Report, June 30, 1982. For a description of the function and makeup of the ICCR, see Thomas Oden, *Conscience and Dividends: The Churches and the Multinationals* (Washington: Ethics and Public Policy Center, forthcoming 1985), chapter 3.

14. See Timothy Smith, "Churches and Corporate Responsibility," in Michael Novak and John W. Cooper, eds., *The Corporation: A Theological Inquiry* (Washington: American Enterprise Institute, 1981), pp. 61-62.

15. Ibid., p. 63; cf. Oden, *Conscience and Dividends,* chapter 2.

16. Interfaith Center on Corporate Responsibility, "Corporate Responsibility Challenges—Spring 1981," *The Corporate Examiner,* January 1981.

17. Howard Schomer, "South Africa: Beyond Fair Employment," *Harvard Business Review,* May-June 1983, p. 146.

18. Interfaith Center on Corporate Responsibility, "Corporate Social Responsibility Challenges, Spring 1983," *The Corporate Examiner,* January/February 1983, pp. 1-3.

19. *The Corporate Examiner,* vol. 12, no. 10 (1983), p. 1.

20. National Council of Churches (NCC) resolution, "Human Rights," December 6, 1963, p. 1.

21. NCC resolution, "Republic of South Africa," June 5, 1964, p. 1.

22. NCC resolution, "Southern Africa," February 23, 1966, p. 26.

23. NCC resolution, "The Church's Policy Toward Southern Africa," December 6, 1972, p. 1.

24. NCC resolution, "The Involvement of IBM in the Republic of South Africa," October 12, 1974, p. 1.

25. NCC resolution, "Southern Africa and U.S. African Policy," October 12, 1975, p. 1.

26. NCC resolution, "Southern Africa," October 9, 1976, p.1.

27. NCC Governing Board statement, "Southern Africa," November 10, 1977.

28. Telephone interview by author with Floyd Robertson of the National Association of Evangelicals, August 5, 1980.

29. Dave Fountain, "Flurry Over the Harvard Corporation's Support of Apartheid," *Sojourners,* June 1978, p. 8.

30. Letter to the author from David M. Howard, February 28, 1983.

31. Ecumenical Ministries of Oregon, "Position Statement Re: Oregon's Public Employee Trust Investments in South Africa," October 21, 1982, pp. 1-2.

32. Community Ministries Commission, Ecumenical Ministries of Oregon, "Background Information on Divestment," September 22, 1982, p. 2.

33. World Peace and Global Affairs Commission, Colorado Council of Churches, "Statement on Opening of an Honorary Consulate by South Africa in Denver," October 28, 1982, pp. 1-2.

34. "American Baptist Resolution Regarding Investment Policies Affected by South African Apartheid," December 1981 (General Board Reference # 8079:12/81).

35. "American Baptist Resolution in Support of the Sullivan Principles," December 1981 (General Board Reference # 8072:12/81).

36. "American Baptist Resolution on the Sullivan Action Plan," December 1981 (General Board Reference # 8079:12/81).

37. Telephone interview with C. J. Malloy by the author, December 20, 1981.

38. Leon H. Sullivan, "It's Time to Step Up the Pressure on South Africa," *Washington Post*, May 10, 1983, p. A19.

39. Ibid.

40. Quoted in Eckehart Lorenz, "The Criteria of *Status Confessionis*," *Lutheran Forum*, Advent 1983, p. 20.

41. Quoted ibid.

42. "World's Lutherans Act Against Apartheid," *New York Times*, August 2, 1984. Cf. William F. Willoughby, "Conclave Tactics Hit," *Washington Times*, August 10, 1984.

43. "Recommendations Passed to Attack Apartheid," news release #84-27 from Lutheran Council in America News Bureau, August 7, 1984, p. 8. Cf. Willmar Thorkelson, "Lutherans Suspend Churches for Accepting Apartheid," *National Catholic Reporter*, August 17, 1984, p. 21.

44. Letters to the author from Eugene W. Linse (Lutheran Church–Missouri Synod), April 7, 1983, and James P. Schaefer (Wisconsin Evangelical Lutheran Synod), February 22, 1983.

45. ALC Church Council, "Goals for Combating Apartheid Through the American Lutheran Church and Its Members," adopted June 25, 1981, in *Apartheid* (Minneapolis: Office of Church in Society, 1981), p. 6.

46. ALC Church Council, "Apartheid in South Africa—Is It Any of Our Business?," ibid., p. 7.

47. Ibid., pp. 1-3.

48. "Response of Lutheran Church in America 1982 Convention to Memorials on Namibia/South Africa," September 10, 1982, p. 2.

49. Ibid., p. 3.

50. Ibid., p. 7.

51. "South Africa: The Search for a Third Way," *Religion and Democracy*, Newsletter of the Institute on Religion and Democracy (Washington, D.C.), January 1983, p. 3.

52. Arthur Keppel-Jones, "Christians and South Africa: The Dilemmas of Responsible Choice," *The Cresset*, January 1982, pp. 9-10.

53. Ibid., p. 13.

54. General Conference of the United Methodist Church, "Southern Africa," Board of Church and Society, Order No. P-117, 1976, p. 2.

55. General Conference of the United Methodist Church, "Southern Africa," Board of Church and Society, Order No. CS7, 1980, p. 2.

56. For an interesting look at the controversy surrounding United Methodist involvement in southern African issues, see a series of *United Methodist Reporter* articles about the church's connection to the "Conference in Solidarity with the Liberation Struggles of the Peoples of Southern Africa," held in October 1981: Roy Howard Beck, "UM Endorsed Event Seemed Controlled by Pro-Soviets," October 23, 1981, with responses and commentaries on October 30, 1981, and November 13, 1981.

57. "Southern Africa," *Daily Christian Advocate* (UMC General Conference), Advance Edition H, March 1, 1984, p. H-58.

58. Ibid., p. H-59.

59. Ibid., pp. H-58, 59.

60. General Conference of the Christian Methodist Episcopal Church, "South Africa Concern," 1978.

61. Letter from Dr. Mance C. Jackson, Jr., to the author, April 13, 1983.

62. *The Presbyterian Layman*, July/August 1983, p. 12.

63. Flaherty, "Revolution, Sayeth the Churchman," p. 31.

64. United Presbyterian General Assembly, "Corporate Social Responsibility: Investment Policy Guidelines," 1971, p. 1.

65. United Presbyterian General Assembly, "Declaration of Conscience on South Africa and Namibia," 1981, pp. v-vi.

66. Ibid., pp. xiii-xiv.

67. Presbyterian Church in the U.S., "Message to the Churches in South Africa," *The Corporate Witness of the General Assembly,* 1977, p. 5.

68. Quoted ibid.

69. Presbyterian Church in the U.S., "Responding to Southern Africa, Commitment to Justice and Reconciliation," *The Corporate Witness of the General Assembly, Public Policy Statements,* 1981, p. 1.

70. Ibid., p. 4.

71. Ibid.

72. Christian Church (Disciples of Christ), "Resolution Concerning Southern Africa" (no. 7757), October 1977.

73. Position paper prepared for Department of Africa, Division of Overseas Ministries, Christian Church (Disciples of Christ), by the Consultation on Southern Africa, March 7-11, 1977, p. 5.

74. Ibid.

75. *The Corporate Examiner,* vol. 12, no. 10 (1983), p. 5.

76. General Brotherhood Board, Church of the Brethren, "Statement on the Republic of South Africa's Apartheid Policies," November 1967, p. 31.

77. Ibid., p. 33.

78. Ibid., p. 34.

79. Episcopal Church Committee on Social Responsibility in Investments, *Annual Report 1980-1981,* p. 1.

80. "The World Demands Sanctions: A Chronology," *Southern Africa,* March 1983, p. 13.

81. Episcopal Church Committee on Social Responsibility in Investments, "Resolution on South Africa," in *Annual Report 1980-1981,* pp. 12-13.

82. Episcopal Church Committee on Social Responsibility in Investments, *Church in Public Affairs—International,* November 1980, p. 3.

83. Ibid., pp. 64, 73.

84. Episcopal Church Committee on Social Responsibility in Investments, *Annual Report 1980-1981,* pp. 15-17.

85. Reformed Church in America, "The Report of the Task Force on Nonviolent Liberation of South Africa," *Minutes of the General Synod,* June 1980, pp. 306-7.

86. Interfaith Center on Corporate Responsibility, "Corporate Responsibility Challenges, Spring 1983," *The Corporate Examiner,* January/February 1983, pp. 2, 6.

87. United Church Boards, *Report to the 12th General Synod of the United Church of Christ on 1977-1979 Corporate Social Responsibility Actions* (New York: United Church Board for World Ministries, 1979), pp. 24-25.

88. Ibid., p. 24.

89. Antonio Chila, "The South African Prime Minister's Mission in Europe," *L'Osservatore Romano* (Weekly Edition in English), July 2, 1984, p. 11.

90. USCC, Committee on Social Development and World Peace, "Southern Africa: Peace or War?," July 7, 1976, in J. Brian Benestad and Francis J. Butler, eds., *Quest for Justice: A Compendium of Statements of the United States Catholic Bishops on the Political and Social Order, 1966-1980* (Washington: USCC, 1981), p. 131.

91. Ibid., pp. 131-32.

92. Telephone interview with J. Bryan Hehir, January 6, 1981.

93. USCC, Administrative Board, "Political Responsibility: Choices for the 1980s," March 22, 1984, p. 11, referring to "USCC Administrative Board Statement on Namibia," 1983.

94. Carole Collins, "Divestment Campaign Makes Gains," *National Catholic Reporter,* February 11, 1983, p. 9.

95. "Proposed Resolution on Archdiocesan Investments Relating to South Africa," approved by Archbishop Rembert Weakland, June 21, 1981, p. 3.

96. "Archdiocese Sells Notes as Protest to Racism," *Catholic Herald Citizen* (Milwaukee), July 9, 1981, p. 1.

97. Letter to the author from Eugene S. Pocernich, director, Office for Human Concerns, Archdiocese of Milwaukee, March 14, 1983.

98. Austin, "Business-Church Accord on South Africa Is Elusive."

99. Rollins Lambert, "Investment in South Africa," *America,* February 12, 1977, p. 131.

100. See James S. Rausch, "Open Letter to the Honorable Henry A. Kissinger," February 7, 1976 (Washington: USCC, 1976).

101. Peter Walshe, "On the Brink in South Africa," *Commonweal,* November 10, 1978, pp. 713-22.

102. Joop Koopman, "South Africa Today," *National Catholic Register,* May 16, 1982, pp. 1, 12.

103. Ibid., p. 12.

104. Letter from Theodore Purcell, S.J., to the author, April 18, 1983.

105. Theodore V. Purcell, S.J., "Reprise of the 'Ethical Investors,' " *Harvard Business Review,* March-April 1980, Reprint No. 80209, pp. 6-7.

106. NCC resolution, "Southern Africa," October 9, 1976, p. 1.

107. Ecumenical Ministries of Oregon, "Position Statement," p. 1.

108. Adrian Kartnycky, "South Africa's Democratic Opposition: An Interview with Chief Buthelezi," *The American Spectator,* March 1983, p. 15.

109. Flaherty, "Revolution, Sayeth the Churchman," p. 32.

110. Michael Novak, "Setting the Record Straight About Racism," *Washington Star,* June 28, 1977, p. A7.

CHAPTER FIVE

1. "How Oppose Apartheid?," *The Christian Century,* May 16, 1984, p. 514.

2. See Richard E. Bissell, *South Africa and the United States: The Erosion of an Influence Relationship* (New York: Praeger Publishers, 1982).

3. Colin Campbell, "More Municipalities Joining Drive to Cut South Africa Links," *New York Times,* September 25, 1984, p. A25.

4. *Bulletin of Statistics,* vol. 13, no. 6 (June 1979); South African Reserve Bank, *Annual Economic Reports 1970-1979* .

5. *Republic of South Africa, House of Assembly Debates* (Hansard), Questions and Replies: March 9, 1979, column 365f; May 11, 1979, column 853f.

6. Statistics cited by Clarence McKee, "A Black American Visits South Africa," *Lincoln Review,* Fall 1982, p. 46.

7. Herman Nickel, "The Case for Doing Business in South Africa," *Fortune,* June 19, 1978, p. 64; reprinted as Essay 12, Ethics and Public Policy Center, 1978.

8. D. A. Etheredge, "South Africa Gold Mines' Case: Good for Labor and Capital," *Financier,* April 1980, p. 50.

9. Allister Sparks, "Botha's Changes Spur Consumerism, Home Ownership in Soweto," *Washington Post,* May 7, 1983, p. A24.

10. Quoted by Clarence McKee in "Oppressor and Oppressed: Knowing the Dif-

ference," speech at Williams College (Williamstown, Mass.), March 6, 1983.

11. Arnt Spandau, *Southern Africa and the Western World* (Reutlingen, FRG: Verlag Harwalik KG, 1984), pp. 45, 49n.

12. Antero Pietila, "Apartheid's Doom May Lie in Numbers," *Baltimore Sun,* April 3, 1983.

13. "Black Power," *The Economist,* December 19, 1981, p. 70.

14. "Labor Relations in South Africa," *Backgrounder* (South African Embassy, Washington, D.C.), December 1982.

15. McKee, "Black American Visits South Africa," p. 46.

16. Neil Ulman, "Growth of Black Unions in South Africa May Bring Political Clout, But Not Now," *Wall Street Journal,* June 20, 1984, p. 35.

17. Ben Roberts, "Black Trade Unionism: A Growing Force in South African Industrial Relations," *South Africa International,* April 1983, p. 292.

18. Ulman, "Growth of Black Unions."

19. Roberts, "Black Trade Unionism," pp. 292-93.

20. For a more complete explanation of "registered" and "unregistered" trade unions, see *South Africa 1984* (Johannesburg: Chris van Rensburg Publications, 1984), chap. 29, esp. pp. 449-70.

21. Quoted in Joseph Lelyveld, "Oppenheimer of South Africa," *New York Times Magazine,* May 8, 1983, p. 35.

22. Ibid.

23. Joseph Lelyveld, "Black Union Flexes Muscles in South Africa Mines," *New York Times,* March 15, 1983, p. A2.

24. Ibid.

25. Michael Sullivan, "S. African Blacks Call Mine Strike," *Washington Times,* September 18, 1984, p. 5A; Robyn Rafel and Steve Mufson, "Black Miners Union in South Africa Wins Modest Concessions by Staging a Walkout," *Wall Street Journal,* September 19, 1984, p. 37.

26. Roberts, "Black Trade Unionism," p. 292.

27. Telegram to Congressman Robert J. Lagomarsino, 1980, quoted in McKee, "Oppressor and Oppressed."

28. Lucy Mvubelo, "My Plea to the I.L.O.," in Hendrik W. van der Merwe et al., eds., *African Perspectives on South Africa* (Stanford, Calif.: Hoover Institution Press, 1978), p. 189.

29. Irving Brown, "A Comment," *AFL-CIO Free Trade Union News,* vol. 37, no. 10 (October 1982), p. 4.

30. Roy Godson, *Black Labor as a Swing Factor in South Africa's Evolution,* International Labor Program Paper no. 3 (Georgetown University, Washington, D.C., Spring 1979), pp. 1-2.

31. Ibid., pp. 3-6.

32. Roberts, "Black Trade Unionism," p. 297.

33. Ibid.

34. Sullivan, "S. African Blacks Call Mine Strike."

35. William B. Gould, "Are Black Unions the Key?," *Commonweal,* November 10, 1978, p. 718.

36. Ulman, "Growth of Black Unions."

37. Robert Conway, "South Africa: Can U.S. Policies Influence Change?," *Worldview,* January 1984, p. 14.

38. Quoted in Helen Zille, "Classes Resume at South African Universities Following Demonstrations at 34 Institutions," *The Chronicle of Higher Education,* October 3, 1984, p. 27.

39. J. P. de Lange, paper delivered at seminar on "The Current Status and Prospects

of the de Lange Committee Recommendations" (Georgetown University Center for Strategic and International Studies, Washington, D.C., May 4, 1983).

40. Thomas J. Bray, "South Africa: Growth and Political Reform," *Wall Street Journal,* September 9, 1982.

41. John Chettle, testimony, *Controls on Exports to South Africa* (U.S. Congress, House, Committee on Foreign Affairs, Subcommittees on International Economic Policy and Trade and on Africa, February 9, 1982) p. 56.

42. K. B. Hartshorne, "Education in South Africa," *The South Africa Foundation News,* September 1984, p. 2.

43. Ibid.

44. Ibid.

45. Howard Schomer, "South Africa: Beyond Fair Employment," *Harvard Business Review,* May-June 1983, p. 151.

46. Samuel P. Huntington, "Will More Countries Become Democratic?," *Political Science Quarterly,* Summer 1984, p. 204.

47. Barrington Moore, Jr., *Social Origins of Dictatorship and Democracy* (Boston: Beacon Press, 1966), p. 418.

48. Walter E. Williams, "Beware the Well-Intentioned," *New York Times,* May 15, 1983.

49. Nickel, "Case for Doing Business," p. 63.

50. Helen Suzman, "What Can America Do? Some Practical Suggestions for Dealing With South Africa," *Washington Post,* March 22, 1984.

51. Lawrence Litvak, Robert DeGrasse, and Kathleen McTigue, *South Africa: Foreign Investment and Apartheid* (Washington: Institute for Policy Studies, 1978), p. 61.

52. Vella Pillay, "Transnationals in South Africa," *Journal of African Marxists,* no. 3 (January 1983), p. 95.

53. "Black Labor in South Africa," *Lincoln Review,* Winter 1980, p. 7.

54. Cited in Nickel, "Case for Doing Business," p. 68.

55. Huntington, "Will More Countries Become Democratic?," p. 204.

56. See, e.g., Michael Novak, *The Spirit of Democratic Capitalism* (New York: Simon and Schuster, 1982), for a general explanation of this role of the market economy.

57. Michael Joseph Smith and Stanley Hoffman, ". . . No, Instead Divest," *New York Times,* June 24, 1983.

58. Litvak, DeGrasse, and McTigue, *South Africa: Foreign Investment and Apartheid,* p. 13.

59. Philip L. Christenson, "United States–South African Economic Relations: Major Issues in the United States," in Alfred O. Hero, Jr., and John Barratt, eds., *The American People and South Africa* (Lexington, Mass.: Lexington Books, 1981), p. 52.

60. Vella Pillay, "Transnationals in South Africa," pp. 106-7.

61. George Melloan, "The Pressures on Apartheid," *Wall Street Journal,* October 29, 1979.

62. Study Commission on U.S. Policy Toward Southern Africa, *South Africa: Time Running Out* (Berkeley: University of California Press, 1981), p. 98.

63. Leon H. Sullivan, "It's Time to Step Up the Pressure on South Africa," *Washington Post,* May 10, 1983, p. A19.

64. Ibid. Cf. Jennifer Davis, "Face It: The Sullivan Principles Haven't Worked," *Washington Post,* May 21, 1983, p. A13.

65. Leon H. Sullivan, "The Sullivan Principles and Change in South Africa," *Africa Report,* May-June 1984, p. 50.

66. Schomer, "South Africa: Beyond Fair Employment," p. 154.

67. Caryle Murphy, "U.S. Firms Pressed on South African Code," *Washington Post,* September 7, 1980.

68. Desaix Myers III, quoted by John Chettle, *Controls on Exports to South Africa,* p. 57.

69. Ibid.

70. Mark Huber, "For U.S. Firms in South Africa, the Threat of Coercive Sullivan Principles," *Institution Analysis,* no. 30, The Heritage Foundation (Washington, D.C.), September 12, 1984, p. 1.

71. Quoted ibid., p. 6.

72. Quoted ibid., p. 7.

73. Michael John Matheson, "Memorandum of Law," May 10, 1983, in *Internal Political Situation in South Africa* (U.S. Congress, House, Committee on Foreign Affairs, Subcommittee on Africa, September 14, 1983), p. 126.

74. Ibid., p. 127.

74. Ibid., p. 127.

75. Ibid., p. 128.

76. Quoted in Huber, "For U.S. Firms in South Africa," p. 9.

77. Quoted ibid.

78. Quoted ibid.

79. Schomer, "South Africa: Beyond Fair Employment," p. 151.

80. "Black Labor in South Africa," p. 4.

81. Ibid., p. 7.

82. Nickel, "Case for Doing Business," p. 63.

83. "South Africa: The Search for a Third Way," *Religion and Democracy,* Newsletter of the Institute on Religion and Democracy (Washington, D.C.), January 1983, p. 3.

84. Adrian Kartnycky, "South Africa's Democratic Opposition: An Interview with Chief Buthelezi," *The American Spectator,* March 1983, pp. 14-15.

85. Ibid., p. 15.

86. Quoted in Allan C. Brownfeld, *South Africa's Importance to the Free World: An Untold Story* (New Rochelle, N.Y.: America's Future, 1984), p. 18.

87. Quoted ibid.

88. Quoted ibid., pp. 18-19.

89. J. N. Reddy, "The Social Responsibility of Business Leaders in South Africa" (paper delivered at seminar on "Dynamics of Development in South Africa," Washington, D.C., October 11, 1983), p. 1.

90. Ibid.

91. Pat Poovalingham, "The Impact of Cultural and Economic Disengagement from South Africa on Intercommunity Relations," in Nic J. Rhoodie, ed., *Conflict Resolution in South Africa* (Pretoria: Institute for Plural Societies, University of Pretoria, 1980), p. 220.

92. Suzanne Garment, "South Africa in Policy Ferment . . . Permanently," *Wall Street Journal,* March 2, 1984.

93. Alan Cowell, "Foes of Apartheid Disputed in Poll; Black South African Factory Workers Oppose Foreign Curbs on Investment," *New York Times,* September 23, 1984, p. 7.

94. Michael Sullivan, "S. Africa Poll: Blacks Oppose U.S. Boycott," *Washington Times,* September 24, 1984, p. 7A.

95. Quoted in Cowell, "Foes of Apartheid Disputed."

96. Ibid.

97. Quoted ibid.

98. Quoted in Sullivan, "S. Africa Poll"; see also Michael Parks, "South African

Blacks' Discontent Increasing," *Los Angeles Times,* September 30, 1984.

99. Quoted in Cowell, "Foes of Apartheid Disputed."

100. Nickel, "Case for Doing Business," p. 60.

101. Conway, "South Africa: Can U.S. Policies Influence Change?," p. 14.

102. Litvak, DeGrasse, and McTigue, *South Africa: Foreign Investment and Apartheid,* p. 81.

103. Bissell, *South Africa and the United States,* pp. 81-82.

104. Arnt Spandau, *Economic Boycott Against South Africa: Normative and Factual Issues* (Cape Town: Juta and Company, 1979), p. 142.

105. John H. Chettle, "Economic Relations Between South Africa and Black Africa," *SAIS Review,* vol. 4, no. 2 (Summer-Fall 1984), p. 131.

106. Quoted ibid.

107. Ibid., p. 123.

108. Shaheen Ayubi et al., *Economic Sanctions in U.S. Foreign Policy* (Philadelphia: Foreign Policy Research Institute, 1982), p.3.

109. Margaret Doxey, *Economic Sanctions and International Enforcement* (New York: Oxford University Press, 1980), cited in Ayubi, *Economic Sanctions,* p. 3.

110. Bissell, *South Africa and the United States,* p. 74.

111. Study Commission on U.S. Policy, *South Africa: Time Running Out,* pp. 134-35.

112. Robert E. Weigand, "Invest in South Africa . . . ," *New York Times,* June 24, 1983.

113. Quoted in Nickel, "Case for Doing Business," p. 70.

CHAPTER SIX

1. Jeane J. Kirkpatrick, "Global Paternalism—The U.N. and the International Regulatory Order," *Regulation,* January-February 1983, p. 21; reprinted as Essay-47, "Global Paternalism: The U.N. and the New International Class Struggle," Ethics and Public Policy Center, 1983.

2. "Black Labor in South Africa," *Lincoln Review,* Winter 1980, p. 37.

3. Kenneth H. W. Hilborn, *South Africa: A Policy for Canada* (Toronto: Citizens for Foreign Aid Reform, 1984), p. 3.

4. Samuel P. Huntington, "Will More Countries Become Democratic?," *Political Science Quarterly,* Summer 1984, p. 213.

5. Robert A. Dahl, *Polyarchy: Participation and Opposition* (New Haven: Yale University Press, 1971), p. 45.

6. Huntington, "Will More Countries Become Democratic?," p. 211.

7. Richard E. Bissell, *South Africa and the United States: The Erosion of an Influence Relationship* (New York: Praeger, 1982), p. 80.

8. Robert J. Hanks, *Southern Africa and Western Security* (Cambridge, Mass.: Institute for Foreign Policy Analysis, 1983), p. 52.

9. Ibid., p. 53.

10. See Ernest W. Lefever, *Amsterdam to Nairobi: The World Council of Churches and the Third World* (Washington: Ethics and Public Policy Center, 1979).

11. "Class Struggle and Identification With the Poor," *Origins,* vol. 14, no. 12 (September 6, 1984), p. 179.

12. "Instruction on Certain Aspects of the 'Theology of Liberation,' " *Origins,* vol. 14, no. 13 (September 13, 1984), p. 203.

13. "Dignity of Human Person and Mankind at Stake," *L'Osservatore Romano* (Weekly Edition in English), July 16, 1984, pp. 11-12.

Bibliography

BOOKS

Analysis of the Interfaith Center on Corporate Responsibility, An. Southport, Conn.: Security Perception Unlimited, 1980.

Appiah-Kubi, Kofi, and Torres, Sergio, eds. *African Theology En Route.* Maryknoll, N.Y.: Orbis Books, 1979.

Ayubi, Shaheen; Bissell, Richard E.; Korsah, Nanu Amu-Brafih; and Lerner, Laurie A. *Economic Sanctions in U.S. Foreign Policy.* Philadelphia: Foreign Policy Research Institute, 1982.

Bissell, Richard E. *South Africa and the United States: The Erosion of an Influence Relationship.* New York: Praeger Publishers, 1982.

Boesak, Allan. *Black and Reformed.* Maryknoll, N.Y.: Orbis Books, 1984.

———. *Walking on Thorns.* Geneva: World Council of Churches, 1984.

Carter, Gwendolen M., and O'Meara, Patrick, eds. *International Politics in Southern Africa.* Bloomington: Indiana University Press, 1982.

Case Against Disinvolvement in the South African Economy, A. Johannesburg: Centre for Business Studies, University of the Witwatersrand, 1980.

Collins, L. John. *Southern Africa: Freedom and Peace.* London: International Defence and Aid Fund for Southern Africa, 1980.

DeGruchy, John W. *The Church Struggle in South Africa.* Grand Rapids, Mich.: Eerdmans, 1979.

DeGruchy, John W., and Villa-Vicencio, Charles, eds. *Apartheid Is a Heresy.* Cape Town: David Philip, 1983; Grand Rapids, Mich.: Eerdmans, 1983.

Department of State, U.S. *Country Reports on Human Rights Practices.* Washington: U.S. Government Printing Office, annual (since 1977).

Gann, L. H., and Duignan, Peter. *South Africa: War, Revolution, or Peace?* Stanford, Calif.: Hoover Institution Press, 1978.

Gastil, Raymond D., ed. *Freedom in the World: Political Rights and Civil Liberties, 1983-1984.* Westport, Conn.: Greenwood Press, 1984.

Gibson, Richard. *African Liberation Movements: Contemporary Struggles Against White Minority Rule.* London: Oxford University Press, 1972.

Gill, David, ed. *Gathered for Life.* Official Report of the Sixth Assembly of the World Council of Churches, Vancouver, British Columbia, 1983. Grand Rapids, Mich.: Eerdmans, 1983.

Hance, William A., ed. *Southern Africa and the United States*. New York: Columbia University Press, 1968.

Hanks, Robert J. *Southern Africa and Western Security*. Cambridge, Mass.: Institute for Foreign Policy Analysis, 1983.

Hero, Alfred O., Jr., and Barratt, John, eds. *The American People and South Africa*. Lexington, Mass: Lexington Books, 1981.

Hope, Marjorie, and Young, James. *The South African Churches in a Revolutionary Situation*. Maryknoll, N.Y.: Orbis Books, 1981.

Isaac, Rael Jean, and Isaac, Erich. *The Coercive Utopians: Social Deception by America's Power Players*. Chicago: Regnery Gateway, 1983.

Jackson, Richard A., ed. *The Multinational Corporation and Social Policy: Special Reference to General Motors in South Africa*. New York: Praeger Publishers, 1974.

Jaster, Robert S. *South Africa's Narrowing Security Options*. Adelphi Papers, no. 159. London: International Institute for Strategic Studies, 1980.

Kitchen, Helen. *U.S. Interests in Africa*. The Washington Papers, 98. New York: Praeger Publishers, 1983.

Kitchen, Helen, and Clough, Michael. *The United States and South Africa: Realities and Red Herrings*. Washington: Center for Strategic and International Studies, 1984.

Knight, Derrick. *Beyond the Pale: The Christian Political Fringe*. Leigh, England: Caraf Publications, 1982.

Lacour-Gayet, Robert. *A History of South Africa*. New York: Hastings House, 1977.

Lefever, Ernest W. *Amsterdam to Nairobi: The World Council of Churches and the Third World*. Washington: Ethics and Public Policy Center, 1979.

Litvak, Lawrence; DeGrasse, Robert; and McTigue, Kathleen. *South Africa: Foreign Investment and Apartheid*. Washington: Institute for Policy Studies, 1978.

Mandela, Nelson. *No Easy Walk to Freedom*. London: Heinemann Educational Books, 1965.

Oden, Thomas C. *Conscience and Dividends: The Churches and the Multinationals*. Washington: Ethics and Public Policy Center, forthcoming (spring 1985).

Parker, Frank J. *South Africa: Lost Opportunities*. Lexington, Mass.: Lexington Books, 1983.

Powers, Charles W. *Social Responsibility and Investments*. Nashville, Tenn.: Abingdon, 1971.

Regehr, Ernie. *Perceptions of Apartheid: The Churches and Political Change in South Africa*. Kitchener, Ontario: Between the Lines, 1979.

Rhoodie, Nic J., ed. *Conflict Resolution in South Africa*. Pretoria: Institute for Plural Societies, 1980.

Schuettinger, Robert L., ed. *South Africa—The Vital Link*. Washington: Council on American Affairs, 1976.

Simon, John G.; Powers, Charles W.; and Gunnemann, Jon P. *The Ethical Investor: Universities and Corporate Responsibility*. New Haven: Yale University Press, 1972.

Sjollema, Baldwin. *Isolating Apartheid*. Geneva: World Council of Churches, Programme to Combat Racism, 1982.

South Africa in the 1980s. 2d ed. London: Catholic Institute for International Relations, 1983.

South Africa 1984: Official Yearbook of the Republic of South Africa. Johannesburg: Chris van Rensburg Publications, 1984.

Spandau, Arnt. *Economic Boycott Against South Africa: Normative and Factual Issues*. Cape Town: Juta and Company, 1979.

—————. *Southern Africa and the Western World (With Special Reference to South Africa)*. Reutlingen, West Germany: Verlag Harwalik KG, 1984.

Study Commission on U.S. Policy Toward Southern Africa. *South Africa: Time Running Out*. Berkeley: University of California Press, 1981.

Tutu, Desmond. *Crying in the Wilderness: The Struggle for Justice in South Africa*. Grand Rapids, Mich.: Eerdmans, 1982.

—————. *Hope and Suffering*. Grand Rapids, Mich.: Eerdmans, 1984.

United Church Boards (United Church of Christ). *Report to the 12th General Synod of the United Church of Christ on 1977-1979 Corporate Social Responsibility Actions*. New York: United Church Board for World Ministries, 1979.

Van der Merwe, Hendrik W; Charton, Nancy C. J.; Kotze, D. A.; and Magnusson, Ake, eds. *African Perspectives on South Africa*. Stanford, Calif.: Hoover Institution Press, 1978.

Waldmann, Raymond J. *Regulating International Business Through Codes of Conduct*. Washington: American Enterprise Institute, 1980.

World Council of Churches, Programme to Combat Racism. *The World Council of Churches and Bank Loans to Apartheid*. Geneva: World Council of Churches, 1977.

ARTICLES

Baker, James E., de St. Jorre, John, and O'Flaherty, J. Daniel. "The American Consensus on South Africa." *Worldview,* October 1979.

Bissell, Richard E. "American Leverage in Southern Africa." *South Africa International,* October 1978.

Cason, James, and Fleshman, Michael. "Dollars for Apartheid." *Multinational Monitor,* November 1983.

Chettle, John H. "Economic Relations Between South Africa and Black Africa." *SAIS Review,* vol. 4, no. 2 (Summer-Fall 1984).

—————. "The Law and Policy of Divestment of South African Stock." *Law and Policy in International Business,* vol. 15, no. 2 (1983).

Crocker, Chester A. "South Africa: Strategy for Change." *Foreign Affairs,* Winter 1980/81.

Frankel, Glenn. "Afrikaners: A Tribe Divided." *Washington Post,* July 29, 30, 31, and August 1, 1984.

Keppel-Jones, Arthur. "Christians and South Africa: The Dilemmas of Responsible Choice." *The Cresset,* January 1982.

Mesenbring, David. "The Two White Races in South Africa." *Worldview,* October 1979.

Mott, William C. "The American Corporation and South Africa." In *Corporate Responsibility: The Viability of Capitalism in an Era of Militant Demands.* Rockford, Ill.: Rockford College Institute, 1978.

Muller, G. S. "Foreign Investment in South Africa." *South Africa International,* October 1978.

Nickel, Herman. "The Case for Doing Business in South Africa." *Fortune,* June 19, 1978.

Norman, Edward. *Politicizing Christianity: Focus on South Africa.* Washington: Ethics and Public Policy Center, 1979.

Novak, Michael. "The Case Against Liberation Theology." *New York Times Magazine,* October 21, 1984.

Obuszewski, Max. "The South African Face Lift." *The Corporate Examiner: ICCR Brief,* vol. 12, no. 10 (1983).

Pillay, Vella. "Transnationals in South Africa." *Journal of African Marxists,* January 1983.

Purcell, Theodore V., S.J. "Management and the 'Ethical' Investors." *Harvard Business Review,* September-October 1979.

—————. "Reprise of the 'Ethical Investors,'" *Harvard Business Review,* March-April 1980.

Sachs, Bernard. "How Hopeless Is South Africa?" *Encounter,* September-October 1984.

Schrire, Robert. "Time Running Out? Rockefeller Commission on United States Policy Towards South Africa." *South Africa International,* October 1981.

Sherman, Stratford P. "Scoring Corporate Conduct in South Africa." *Fortune,* July 9, 1984.

Sincere, Richard E., Jr. "The Churches and Investment in South Africa." *America,* March 3, 1984.

—————. "The Politics of Sentiment: U.S. Churches Approach Investment in South Africa." *South Africa International,* January 1984.

Smith, Timothy. "Churches and Corporate Responsibility." In *The Corporation: A Theological Inquiry,* edited by Michael Novak and John W. Cooper. Washington: American Enterprise Institute, 1981.

Sullivan, Leon H. "The Sullivan Principles and Change in South Africa." *Africa Report,* May-June, 1984.

Thomas, David. "Church-State Relations in South Africa: Uncomfortable Bedfellows." *South Africa International,* July 1982.

Villa-Vicencio, Charles. "The Church: Discordant and Divided." *Africa Report,* July-August 1983.

Willers, David. "South Africa: The Disinvestment Debate." *Africa Report,* September-October 1982.

Williams, Oliver, C.S.C. "Who Cast the First Stone?" *Harvard Business Review,* September-October 1984.

Zille, Helen. "Survey of Black Workers in South Africa Finds that Most Oppose Cuts in Foreign Investments." *Chronicle of Higher Education,* November 21, 1984.

Index of Names